Essential JavaScript Concepts To Learn for Beginner and Intermediate Developers

By: Roggie Clark

Learn HTML, CSS, and JavaScript With This One Book

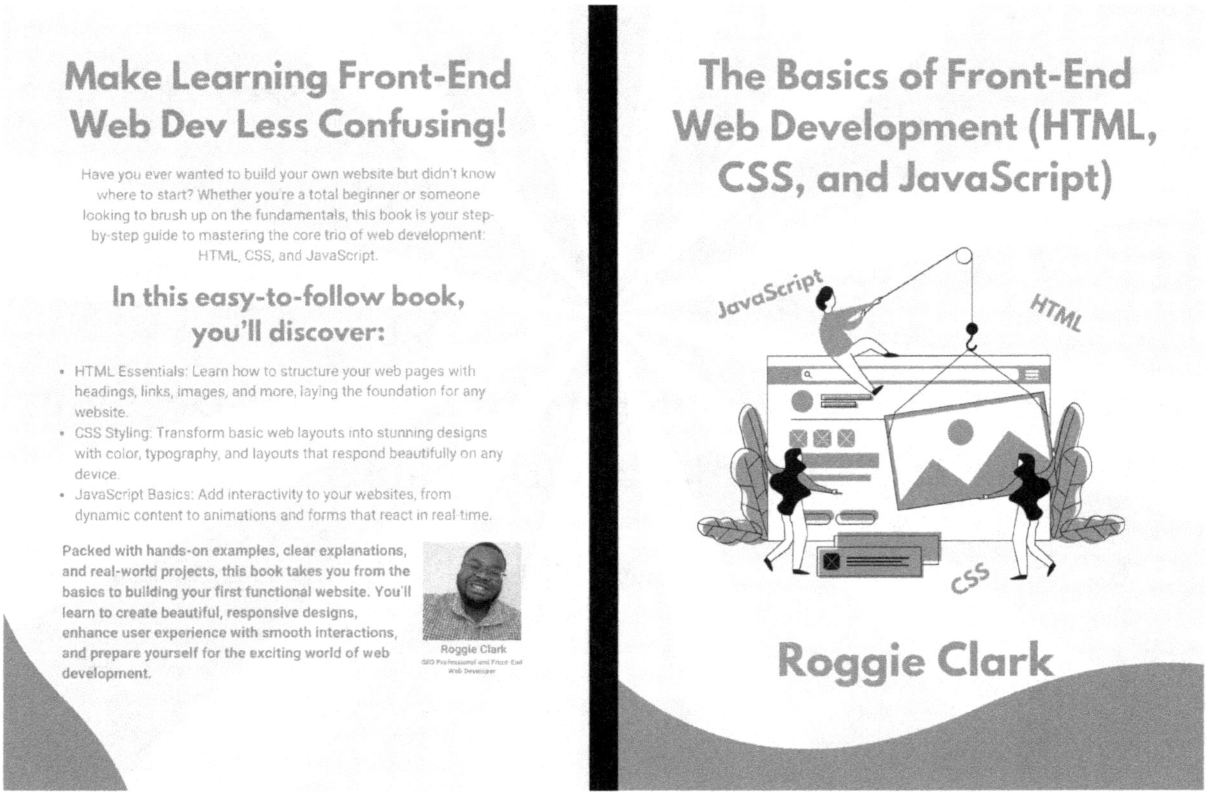

To learn all three coding languages, checkout the full book.

https://www.amazon.com/Basics-Front-End-Development-HTML-JavaScript-ebook/dp/B0DJ147B15

Learn HTML With This Book

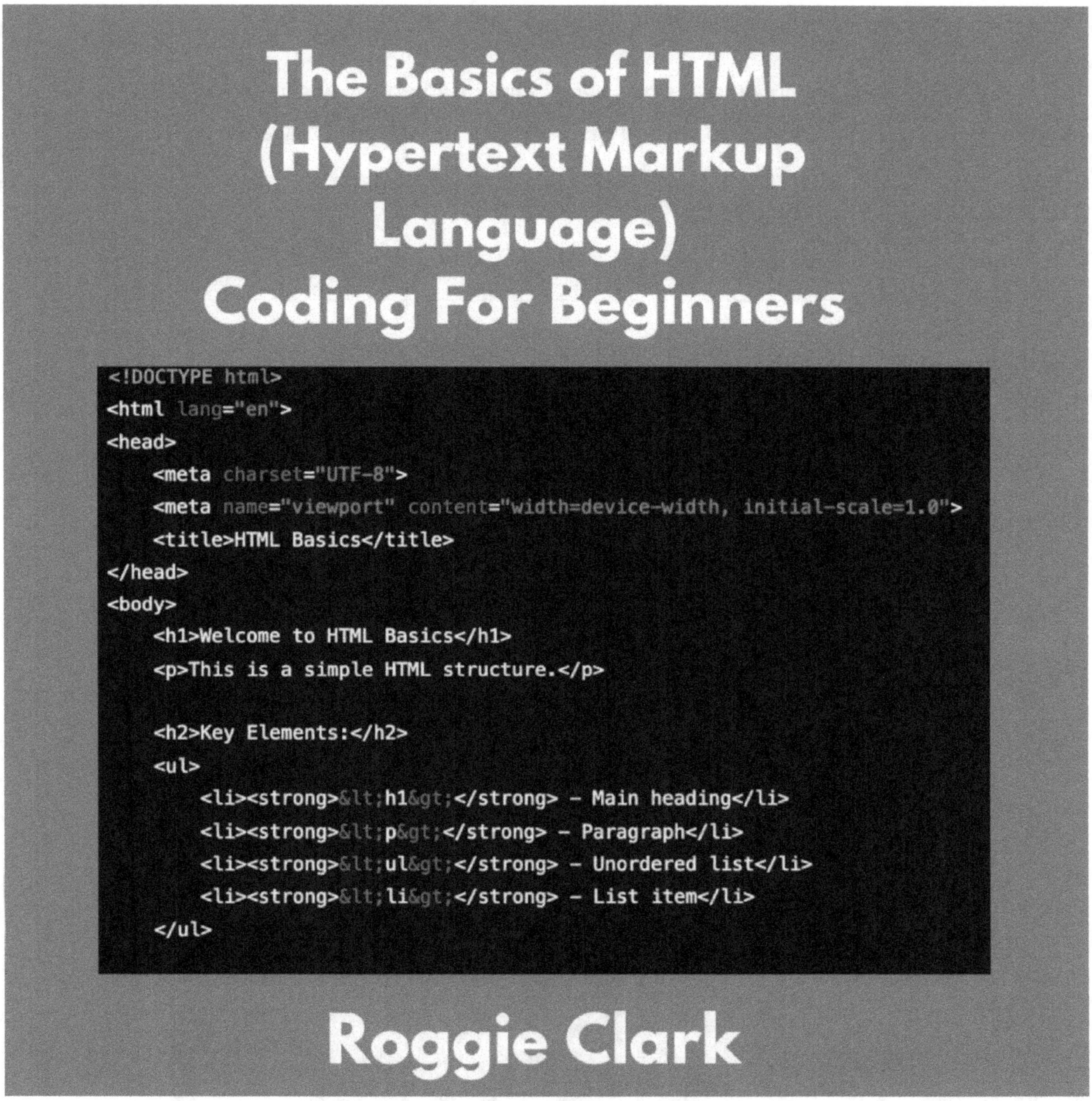

Learn how to write HTML code by getting this book.

https://www.amazon.com/Basics-Hypertext-Markup-Language-Beginners-ebook

Learn SEO Too

Learning front-end web development is only half the battle to producing an amazing web experience. Also, you need to learn **SEO (search engine optimization)**.

Learning SEO ensures that visitors can actually find your website and apps on the internet. Below I included links to several SEO books I've written. They are excellent reads.

The ABCs of SEO: Search Engine Optimization 101

https://www.amazon.com/ABCs-Search-Engine-Optimization-Page-ebook/dp/B0C2JSLW7M

The Technical SEO Handbook

https://www.amazon.com/Technical-SEO-Handbook-Learn-Issues-ebook/dp/B0CMBJR9QV

The SEO and Web Developer Collaboration Guide

https://www.amazon.com/SEO-Web-Developer-Collaboration-Guide-ebook/dp/B0DHLBM48C

Copyright

Title: Essential JavaScript Concepts To Learn for Beginner and Intermediate Developers
Author: Roggie Clark

Cover Design: Roggie Clark
Editing: Renee' Clark

Printed in the United States of America

Disclaimer

The views and opinions expressed in this book are those of the author and do not necessarily reflect the official policy or position of any individual, company, or organization cited or referenced in the text.

The author is not affiliated with any of the individuals, companies, or organizations mentioned in the text, nor does the author receive any form of compensation for citing or referencing them. Some sample scenarios in this text are fictitious. Any similarity to actual persons, living or dead, is coincidental.

The professional information (strategies, tips, and concepts) in this text is distributed on an "as is" basis, without warranty. While every precaution has been taken in the preparation of the text to ensure all information is accurate, neither the author nor the publisher shall have any liability to any person or entity with respect to any loss or damage caused or alleged to be caused directly or indirectly by the instructions contained in this text or by the computer software and hardware products described in it.

Neither the author nor the publisher guarantees any specific results or outcomes, and the information provided in this text should not be construed as professional advice. Readers should always consult with a qualified professional before making any significant changes to their website or business.

By reading this text, you agree that the author nor the publisher is responsible for any direct, indirect, incidental, or consequential damages that may arise from the use of the information provided. You assume full responsibility for any actions taken based on the information presented in this text.

Table of Contents

Chapter 1: Introduction

Websites and mobile apps today offer far more for users to see than just static text and images. The modern web is filled with interactive elements such as buttons that respond visually, animations that enhance usability, dropdown menus that make navigation a breeze, and forms that validate user input instantly.

These dynamic features, which bring websites and mobile applications to life, are all made possible through **JavaScript**. This versatile and powerful programming language transforms static web pages into engaging experiences that captivate users. Without JavaScript, the web would be limited to dull, static content. With it, you can create rich, exciting interfaces that respond instantly to user actions and update web content in real-time, no page reloads necessary. How cool is that?

Moreover, JavaScript's reach extends beyond just websites. It powers countless web-based applications, mobile apps via frameworks like React Native, server-side development through Node.js, APIs (Application Programming Interfaces), and even desktop applications. This universality makes JavaScript one of the most versatile and widely used programming languages in the world.

If you've ever spoken with web developers, you know that JavaScript is their bread and butter, right alongside **HTML** and **CSS**. Can you really call yourself a front-end developer without knowing at least some JavaScript? I don't think so! Even as an SEO and digital marketing professional, I found that understanding JavaScript significantly boosted my ability to optimize websites and collaborate more effectively with website developers. For anyone in the digital marketing sphere or any role connected to web technology, learning JavaScript is a game-changer.

Beyond the technical perks, mastering JavaScript can also open doors to new opportunities. Whether you want to enhance your current role or pivot into web development, JavaScript skills are highly sought after. By learning it, you're investing in your professional growth and increasing your value in the digital economy. Plus, the satisfaction that comes from building something interactive and functional on the web is truly rewarding.

This book will introduce you to JavaScript in a clear, straightforward way. You'll start with the fundamentals and gradually explore some intermediate concepts, equipping you with the tools you need to start creating your own interactive web pages. While this book doesn't cover every aspect of JavaScript, since the language evolves constantly, what you'll learn here will give you a strong foundation you can build on for years to come. This isn't just some wordy guide you find on Google, no, this is a real book that you can keep for a lifetime.

By the end of this book, you'll be confident in creating interactive web applications that grab attention and deliver memorable user experiences. Whether your goal is to build responsive forms, dynamic animations, or more complex applications, JavaScript offers the power and flexibility to bring your ideas to life, and this book will guide you every step of the way.

If you're ready, buckle up and get excited, your journey into JavaScript begins here. Turn to the next page to get started!

Chapter 2: JavaScript Basics

Before you can build interactive features, write complex logic, or master advanced syntax, you need to understand the basics, the core building blocks that make JavaScript function. Think of this as learning the alphabet before writing full sentences. This section is your entry point, even if you've never written a single line of code.

We'll begin by exploring what JavaScript is, its history, how it fits into the world of web development alongside HTML and CSS, and how it allows you to communicate instructions to a webpage. Also, we'll take a look at **ECMAScript**, the official standard that defines how JavaScript is developed and maintained. JavaScript is constantly evolving, and ECMAScript helps guide that evolution. You'll gain insight into how new features are proposed and adopted, what role ECMAScript plays in shaping the language, and why keeping up with its updates matters as you grow as a developer.

You'll also learn about the basics of **JavaScript Syntax**, or the unique set of rules that govern how you write code, **how to insert JavaScript into an HTML file**, and how the browser interprets the code you write. This early exposure will give you the confidence to start writing code with clarity and purpose.

Think of this chapter as helping to build your JavaScript toolbox. Once it's full of these essential tools, you'll be ready to construct programs with real functionality. With that said, let's get started.

JavaScript's Creation

In the early days of the internet, websites were largely static and uninspiring, much like a simple poster hanging on a wall. They displayed text and images but lacked interactivity, animation, or dynamic content. Users could not play games, watch videos seamlessly, or interact with engaging elements such as buttons or pop-ups. The web experience was limited to passive consumption rather than active engagement.

This all changed in 1995, when **Brendan Eich**, a talented programmer working at Netscape, was tasked with transforming the web into a more interactive and user-friendly environment. Netscape was one of the pioneering companies behind early web browsers, the software applications that enable us to access and navigate websites. Legend has it, Eich was given an ambitious deadline: just 10 days to develop a scripting language that could enable web pages to respond dynamically to user actions, process input, and display animations or other effects.

Eich rose to the challenge, designing a language initially called *Mocha*, which was later renamed **JavaScript** to capitalize on the popularity of the term "Java" at the time. This new language empowered websites to become much more than static documents. With JavaScript, web pages could respond to clicks, validate form inputs instantly, run animations, and even support interactive games and applications.

Today, JavaScript is a foundational technology of the web, responsible for the dynamic, interactive experiences that users have come to expect. It enables everything from simple button clicks to complex applications running directly in the browser. Much like constructing with building blocks, each element of JavaScript has a unique role that, when combined, enables the creation of sophisticated and engaging web experiences.

Key Properties of JavaScript

One of the defining features that sets JavaScript apart from many other programming languages is how it runs. Unlike languages such as Java or C++, which are typically compiled ahead of time and executed by a separate application, JavaScript is executed directly in the user's web browser. This makes JavaScript an **interpreted language**, and more specifically, a **Just-In-Time (JIT) compiled** language.

What does that mean in plain English? It means JavaScript is processed and run on the fly, right as the browser encounters it, rather than needing to be translated into machine code beforehand. This allows developers to write dynamic code that can be immediately tested and seen in action, which is one reason JavaScript is such a popular tool for creating fast, interactive user experiences.

Another core property of JavaScript is how it executes code: by default, JavaScript runs **synchronously**. That means the browser reads and executes each line of code in the exact order it appears, one line after another. If a task takes a long time to complete (like loading data from a server), it can delay everything else from running.

However, JavaScript also supports **asynchronous** execution. This allows time-consuming tasks to run in the background, so the rest of the page can continue loading and responding to user input without getting stuck. Features like `setTimeout`, `fetch`, and **Promises** make asynchronous programming in JavaScript both possible and practical. We will explore these features in depth in the chapters that follow.

This ability to combine synchronous and asynchronous behavior gives web developers the flexibility to build **dynamic, responsive** websites and applications. For example, like I said in chapter 1, JavaScript can help a page to fetch new content without reloading, validate a form in real time, or display animations that react to user interactions—all thanks to JavaScript.

In short, JavaScript's key properties, **interpreted execution, synchronous/asynchronous control,** and **browser-native behavior**, make it a uniquely powerful language for creating modern, engaging web experiences.

ECMAScript

If you didn't know, **ECMAScript** is the standard language behind JavaScript development. It is used to ensure that JavaScript can be run on a variety of web browsers. Here's some more detail to build on that:

ECMAScript (often abbreviated as ES) is a scripting language specification standardized by *ECMA International (the European Computer Manufacturers Association)*. It defines the core features, syntax, and semantics for scripting languages like JavaScript.

JavaScript is an implementation of the ECMAScript specification. While JavaScript is the name of the programming language used primarily in browsers, ECMAScript is the formal specification that JavaScript engines follow. Other languages like JScript and ActionScript also implement ECMAScript to various extents, but we are not focusing on those languages for this book.

Before ECMAScript standards, browsers implemented JavaScript features differently, causing inconsistencies and compatibility problems. ECMAScript standardizes how the language should behave so that scripts run consistently across different browsers and environments.

ES6, officially called ECMAScript 2015 , was a major update that introduced many new features, making JavaScript more powerful and easier to write. While there are numerous updated versions of ECMAScript, as a new update is released every year, many professional developers still recommend ES6 as a good place to start for beginners. So when I am discussing JavaScript concepts in this book, they are geared towards ES6. Let's discuss a bit more deeply about the intricacies of JavaScript by looking at its *Syntax*.

JavaScript Syntax

JavaScript Syntax refers to the set of rules that define how JavaScript code must be written in order to be correctly interpreted and executed by the browser. Just like grammar in a spoken language, syntax in programming ensures that your instructions make sense to the interpreter, in this case, the browser's JavaScript engine.

- One of the most important aspects of JavaScript syntax is that it is **case-sensitive**. This means that changing the capitalization of letters will completely change how your code is interpreted. For instance, `FirstName` and `firstname` would be treated as two entirely different variables. Failing to match case consistently is a common beginner error, so it's something to watch out for early on.
- JavaScript also uses the **Unicode character set**, which allows developers to write code using letters, symbols, and characters from virtually any language in the world. This is especially useful in international applications where variable names or content might need to support non-English languages or special characters.
- Another element of JavaScript syntax is the use of **semicolons (`;`)** to end statements. While JavaScript does not require semicolons at the end of every line due to a feature called *automatic semicolon insertion*, many developers still use them for clarity and consistency. That said, omitting semicolons has become increasingly popular in modern JavaScript style guides, especially when using newer syntax supported by frameworks and tools that manage code formatting automatically.
- JavaScript syntax also includes **brackets `{}` for code blocks, parentheses `()` for function arguments**, and **square brackets `[]` for arrays**. Understanding when and how to use these symbols is key to writing clear and functional code.

While we're only scratching the surface here, mastering these basic rules is essential for moving on to more complex structures like loops, conditionals, and functions. In the next chapter, we'll dive deeper into JavaScript syntax and explore how to write more structured and functional programs.

Strict Mode

I can't mention syntax without mentioning the importance of using **Strict Mode**. This is a more intermediate concept, but I think it's worth mentioning here. While JavaScript is known for being flexible, that flexibility can sometimes allow for risky or error-prone behavior to go unnoticed. To help developers write cleaner and more secure code, JavaScript offers strict mode, a way to opt into a restricted variant of the language that enforces stricter parsing and error handling.

`"use strict";` helps catch errors and prevent unsafe actions:

Strict mode is enabled by placing `"use strict";` at the beginning of a script or function. When in strict mode, JavaScript will throw errors for practices that are otherwise silently ignored. This includes things like assigning values to undeclared variables, using reserved keywords incorrectly, or creating duplicate function parameters.

Example:

```
"use strict";

x = 3.14; // ReferenceError: x is not defined
```

Without strict mode, this code would have created a global variable `x` unintentionally. With strict mode, JavaScript alerts the developer to the mistake. So, the developer needs to go back and declare the variable `x`.

Strict mode also disables some features that are considered problematic or confusing, such as `with` statements, and can make debugging easier by catching subtle bugs earlier in development.

Using `"use strict";` is a best practice for improving code reliability and safety. It encourages better habits, prevents common errors, and lays the foundation for future-proof JavaScript code.

How JavaScript is Added to an HTML Document

Before you can start writing JavaScript code, it is also important to know how JavaScript can be deployed to HTML pages. JavaScript can be implemented on web pages in one of three ways:

1. **Internally**
2. **Externally**
3. **Inline**

Each has its own pros and cons.

Internal JavaScript

If JavaScript is written directly in an HTML document, a `<script>` tag in the `<head>` section of the document with the `language` and `type` attributes added indicates the code has been added.

Here's an example:

```
<head>
     <script language = "javascript" type = "text/javascript">
(function (w, d, s, l, i) {
        w[l] = w[l] || [];
        w[l].push({ "gtm.start": new Date().getTime(), event:
"gtm.js" });
        var f = d.getElementsByTagName(s)[0],
          j = d.createElement(s),
          dl = l != "dataLayer" ? "&l=" + l : "";
        j.async = true;
        j.src = "https://www.googletagmanager.com/gtm.js?id=" +
i + dl;
        f.parentNode.insertBefore(j, f);
      })(window, document, "script", "dataLayer", "GTM-
KVL636G");

     </script>
</head>
```

As you can see, the code snippet is *nested* inside the `<head>` tags, and the`language` and `type` attributes were added to the `<script>` tag to indicate that a JavaScript code snippet is being added. The "code" nested in the `<script>` tag is an example of a *tracking pixel,* which is a piece of JavaScript code used to track a webpage user's actions on the page.

Pros and Cons

Pros:

- Generally takes up less space

Cons:

- If in the `<head>` section, it can slow down the webpage (render-blocking)
- It may be harder to maintain and reuse code

External JavaScript

The code can also be loaded through an *external* file with the `.js` extension and then loading it within the page with again a `<script>` tag, and an [`src`] attribute added to the script tag here's an example:

```
<body>
    <script src="name of file.js"></script>
</body>
```

The code does not necessarily need to be nested in the `<head>` tag. In this case, the code is being loaded from the `<body>` section of the HTML document.

Here are some pros and cons of external JavaScript:

Pros and Cons

Pros:

- Easy to reuse code.
- Easier to read
- Easier to compress and minify

Cons:

- The browser has to make an extra HTTP request to get the `.js` code.
- Code can be downloaded using the URL of the `.js` file. This can help coders steal your code easily.
- If two `.js` files are dependent on one another, then a failure in one file may affect the execution of the other dependent file.
- A small change to a common `.js` file may cause unexpected results in some of the HTML files.

Inline JavaScript

Lastly, you can add the JavaScript code *inline* or directly inside an HTML tag, and then add **attributes** to the tag that trigger an action when interacted with, such as:

- `onclick` (when the object is clicked on by the user)
- `onmouseover` (when the user moves their mouse)
- `onkeypress` (when the user presses a specific key on their keyboard)
- `onload` (when the user loads the webpage), etc.

These are also considered to be examples of **JavaScript Events** (we will explore this in chapter 4.)

Here's an example:

```
<button onclick="alert('Hello World!')">Click Me</button>
```

As you can see the attribute `onclick` was added with the action to show a display box with the text “Hello world” when the button is clicked on.

Here are the Pros and Cons of this method:

Pros and Cons

Pros:

- Generally takes up less space

Cons:

- Harder to maintain code
- Difficult to reuse code for other projects
- Unable to be *cached* or saved for future use by Web Browsers

So, as you can see, there are numerous ways to add JavaScript to your webpages. Again, this is important to know so that you are not stuck or confused about where to start.

DOM (Document Object Model) Manipulation

You can’t mention how to add JavaScript to HTML without mentioning the DOM. The **Document Object Model (DOM)** represents the structure of a webpage as a tree of objects. Each element on the page is part of this tree. JavaScript allows you to access and manipulate the DOM, which enables dynamic updates to the HTML content. You can use the graphic I included below from Wikipedia to help you make sense of the DOM.

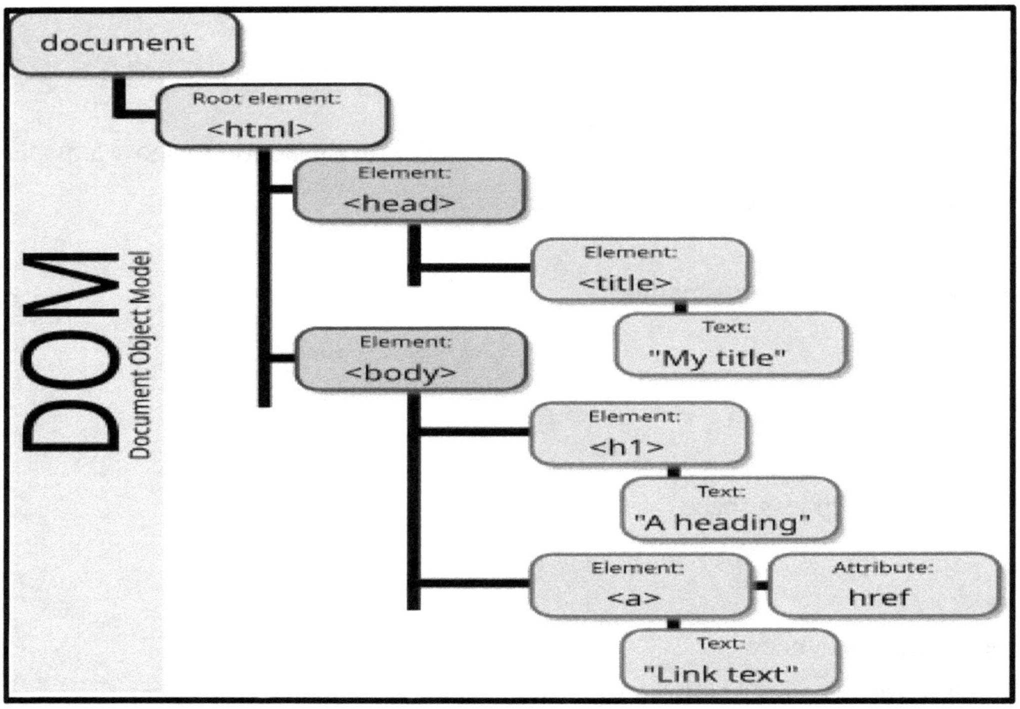

Cited From: https://en.wikipedia.org/wiki/Document_Object_Model

Let's go over the diagram step by step:

1. `document`

- This is the **topmost object** in the DOM.
- In JavaScript, everything starts from `document`.

Example:

```
console.log(document);
```

---

2. `<html>` (Root Element)

- The root of the HTML document.
- Everything on the page — head and body — is inside this.

Access it with:

```
document.documentElement
```

---

3. `<head>` and `<body>` (Children of `<html>`)

- These are the two **main branches** of the HTML.
- `<head>` holds metadata like `<title>`, CSS, etc.
- `<body>` holds visible content like headings, links, etc.

Access:

```
document.head

document.body
```

---

4. `<title>` inside `<head>`

- Represents the text shown in the browser tab.
- Text node `"My title"` is a **child** of `<title>`.

Access or modify:

```
document.title = "New Title";
```

---

5. `<h1>` inside `<body>`

- This is a heading element.

- Contains the text node `"A heading"`.

Access:

```
const heading = document.querySelector("h1");

heading.textContent = "Updated Heading";
```

---

6. `<a>` (Anchor Element) inside `<body>`

- This is a link.
- It has:
    - A **text node**: `"Link text"`
    - An **attribute**: `href`, which defines the link target.

Access or modify:

```
const link = document.querySelector("a");

link.href = "https://example.com";

link.textContent = "Visit Example";
```

As you can see, the DOM (Document Object Model) is a tree-like structure that represents an HTML document in memory. Each HTML element becomes a **node**, including elements, text, and attributes, allowing JavaScript to access and manipulate the page dynamically. Starting from the `document` root, JavaScript can read and modify elements like `<title>`, `<h1>`, and `<a>` to change content, styles, or behavior in real time.

Here are some additional things you can do with DOM manipulation. For example, you can:

- Change the content of an element.

- Modify the styles dynamically.
- Add or remove elements from the page.

Let's look at an example of DOM manipulation in action:

```
document.getElementById("heading").innerHTML = "New Heading Text";
```

This line of JavaScript will change the content of an HTML element with the ID `heading` to `"New Heading Text"`. As you can see, DOM manipulation is an excellent way to bring static webpages to life.

Last Thoughts

Like I said, the point of this chapter was to help you begin to lay the foundation of what JavaScript is all about. The goal was to help you see that JavaScript can be a very simple language to use and understand, as long as you understand the rules and what you can and can not do with it.

This will save you time debugging and ensure that you write code that can be accurately deciphered by other developers. In the next section, we are going to dive in deeper, by discussing the fundamental components that make up the JavaScript language.

Chapter 3: Fundamental JavaScript Concepts

JavaScript has a specific syntax, which refers to the rules and structure the language follows, like grammar in spoken language. But beyond syntax, there are fundamental building blocks that give JavaScript its power and flexibility. These include **Values**, **Literals**, **Variables**, **Data types**, **Operators**, **Statements**, **Expressions**, and **Comments**. There are also more detailed, but still fundamental concepts like functions, events, conditional statements, and loops, but I will discuss those in their own specific sections because they can get pretty technical.

While these concepts all rely on proper syntax to work correctly, they are not syntax themselves. Instead, they are core components of the JavaScript language, essential tools that allow developers to write logic, interact with web pages, and control how programs behave. Understanding each of these components is key to becoming fluent in JavaScript and building interactive, dynamic websites. By the end of this section, you'll be able to say with confidence:

- "I know what kind of data I'm working with."
- "I understand how to organize it."
- "And I know how to make it do what I want."

Essentially, you will start to know enough that you can at least write some basic JavaScript code that is accurate and complete. Let's get started shall we?

Values

In JavaScript, **Values** can be thought of as pieces or chunks of information that are assigned to different numbers or pieces of text. In JavaScript, two of the most common values are **Literals** and **Variables**.

- **Fixed values** - Literals
- **Changeable values** - Variables

I am going to explain each of these values in more detail below.

Literals

Fixed values are also referred to as **Literals**, they are called "fixed values" because they are values that generally are not changed. Once they are declared, they remain as such. They can be **Numbers** written either with or without decimals, like:

```
9.20

9001
```

Or **Strings,** which are text, written within double or single quotes:

```
"John Doe"

'John Doe'
```

Both types of values can be used to store pieces of information. There are additional *Data Types* like **Boolean, Array, Objects,** and **Symbols,** which are standalone entities or things with their own identity and properties. We will explore *Data Types* in more detail in their own section.

Each of these can be used to represent values as well, but Fixed values and strings are the most simplistic, and can help you establish a foundation for exploring more intricate values in the future.

Variables

As I mentioned**, Variables** are changeable values. A Variable can be declared using var, let, and const keywords. Let's explore each of these in more detail.

- var is a more archaic way to define a JavaScript variable. It has fallen out of use because it can cause confusion with other JavaScript keywords, and it has limited usage due to Scoping issues.

- let removes the confusion and error of var. It is the new and recommended way of declaring variables in JavaScript. Especially, in ES6.

- const is used to declare a constant variable that cannot be changed once assigned a value.

Variables can also be thought of as digital containers for holding Literal values. Revisiting the last example, here are variables written with numbers:

```
var x = 5;

let y = 6;

const z = x + y;
```

As you can see, the keywords `var`, `let`, and `const`, are used to designate variables. Additionally, in the code snippet, **operators** are used to perform mathematical and logical operations between variables, as you can see the operators = and + were used. I will explain this concept and the code snippet in more detail in the *Operator section.*

Data Types

As I mentioned, in addition to Numbers, Literal Values and Variables can be represented by different *Data Types*, more specifically, each Data Type can fall into one of two categories, **Primitive** and **Structured**.

Primitive Data Types

Primitive types are the most basic, **immutable** (cannot be changed), and are **copied by value**. These types hold a single value and are not objects. The primitive data types are as follows: `String`, `Number`, `Boolean`, `Undefined`, `Null`, `Symbol`, and `BigInt`, which represent single, immutable values. Let's break down these types one by one:

1. String:

A sequence of characters used to represent text.

Example:

```
let greeting = "Hello, World!";
console.log(greeting); // Output: Hello, World!
```

---

2. Number:

Represents both integer and floating-point numbers, i.e. digits like 123

Example:

```
let age = 30;
let pi = 3.14;
console.log(age); // Output: 30
console.log(pi);  // Output: 3.14
```

---

3. Boolean:

Represents logical entities, having only two values: `true` or `false`.

Example:

```
let isDeveloper = true;
console.log(isDeveloper); // Output: true
```

---

4. Undefined:

A variable that has been declared but not yet assigned a value.

Example:

```
let notAssigned;
console.log(notAssigned); // Output: undefined
```

---

5. Null:

Represents the intentional absence of any object value.

Example:

```
let emptyValue = null;
console.log(emptyValue); // Output: null
```

---

6. Symbol:

A unique and immutable primitive value, often used as a key in object properties.

Example:

```
let sym = Symbol("uniqueKey");
```

```
let obj = {
  [sym]: "value"
};
console.log(obj[sym]); // Output: value
```

---

7. BigInt

A unique and immutable primitive value, introduced in ES11 for arbitrarily large integers.

Example:

```
let bigNumber = 1234567890123456789012345678901234567890n;
console.log(bigNumber);
```

Structured Data Types

On the other hand, the **Structured (or non-primitive) data types** include `Object`, and `Array`. Also, it includes `Function` and other built-in object types like `Map`, and `Set`, which are used to store collections of values and more complex data structures. But we will again explore those later in the book because they are just too technical and confusing to tackle right here in the book.

1. Array:

An ordered list of values, or that can be referenced by name i.e. a collection of items (indexed elements).

Example:

```
let colors = ["red", "green", "blue"];
console.log(colors[1]); // Output: green
```

---

2. Object:

A collection of key-value pairs.

Example:

```
let person = {
  name: "Alice",
  age: 25,
  isStudent: false
};
console.log(person.name); // Output: Alice
```

Those are all the data types that we are going to be exploring for right now, but like I said will dive into more intricate ones later in the book. Now let's move on to another fundamental concept, and that is Operators.

Operators

An **Operator** is a symbol that is used to perform a mathematical or logical operation between variables or values. Here's the code snippet example I referenced in the *Variable section*:

```
var x = 5;

var y = 6;

var z = x + y;
```

The symbol = is used to represent the **assignment operator,** which is used to assign values to a specific symbol. In this case, it is used to show that the **letter X** is equal to 5 and the **letter Y** is equal to 6.

Also, the assignment operator is used in conjunction with the **addition operator** + to show that the **letter *Z*** is equal to the sum of letters **X** and **Y**.

There are other *arithmetic operators* such as:

Arithmetic operators

1. Subtraction (-):

Description: Subtracts the right-hand operand from the left-hand operand.

Example:

```
let result = 10 - 5; // result is 5
```

Explanation: Here, `10 - 5` equals `5`. The `-` operator simply subtracts the right-hand operand value of `5` from the left-hand operand value of `10`.

---

2. Multiplication Operator (*)

Description: The multiplication operator is used to multiply two numbers.

Example:

```
let a = 6;

let b = 4;

let result = a * b; // Multiplies 6 by 4

console.log(result); // Output: 24
```

Explanation: Here, `6 * 4` equals `24`. The `*` operator simply multiplies the two numbers on either side of it.

---

3. Division (/):

Description: Divides the left-hand operand by the right-hand operand.

Example:

```
let result = 10 / 2; // result is 5
```

Explanation: Here, `10 / 2` equals `5`. The `/` operator simply divides the left-hand operand `10` by the right-hand operand `2`.

---

4. Modulus (`%`):

Description: Returns the remainder of the division between two numbers.

Example:

```
let result = 10 % 3; // result is 1
```

Explanation: Here, `10 % 3` equals `1`. The `%` operator simply divides the left-hand operand `10` by the right-hand operand `3`. Because `10` divided by `3` gives a remainder of `1` the answer is `1`

Comparison Operators

Comparison operators help you perform logical comparisons in your JavaScript code, allowing you to control the flow of execution based on conditions. Here they are:

1. Equality (`==`)

Description: Compares two values for equality after converting them to a common type (type coercion).

Example:

```
console.log(5 == '5'); // true
```

Here, the string '5' is converted to a number before comparison.

---

2. Inequality (!=)

Description: Compares two values for inequality after type coercion.

Example:

```
console.log(5 != '6'); // true
```

The values are not equal, so it returns true.

---

3. Strict Equality (===)

Description: Compares two values for equality without type conversion (no coercion).

Example:

```
console.log(5 === '5'); // false
```

Here, the comparison fails because the types (number vs. string) are different.

---

4. Strict Inequality (!==)

Description: Compares two values for inequality without type conversion.

Example:

```
console.log(5 !== '5'); // true
```

The values are not equal due to different types, so it returns true.

---

5. Less Than (<)

Description: Checks if the left operand is less than the right operand.

Example:

```
console.log(5 < 10); // true
```

---

6. Greater Than (>)

Description: Checks if the left operand is greater than the right operand.

Example:

```
console.log(10 > 5); // true
```

---

7. Less Than or Equal To (<=)

Description: Checks if the left operand is less than or equal to the right operand.

Example:

```
console.log(5 <= 5); // true
```

---

8. Greater Than or Equal To (>=)

Description: Checks if the left operand is greater than or equal to the right operand. `==` and `!=`: Perform type coercion (we will explore *Type coercion*, and other typing systems in their own section later).

- `===` and `!==`: No type coercion; strict checks.

- `<`, `>`, `<=`, `>=`: Compare numerical values.

These operators help you perform logical comparisons in your JavaScript code, allowing you to control the flow of execution based on conditions.

Example:

```
console.log(10 >= 5); // true
```

Logical Operators

Logical operators are used to combine or invert Boolean values. The three main logical operators are:

Logical AND (`&&`):

Description: This operator returns `true` if both operands are true.

Example:

```
const a = true;

const b = false;

const result = a && b; // result is false
```

Explanation: Here, result is `false` because both `a` and `b` must be true for the result to be `true`.

Logical OR (`||`):

Description: This operator returns `true` if at least one of the operands is true.

Example:

```
const a = true;

const b = false;

const result = a || b; // result is true
```

Explanation: In this case, result is `true` because `a` is true, so the overall expression evaluates to true.

Logical NOT (`!`):

Description: This operator inverts the boolean value of its operand.

Example:

```
const a = true;

const result = !a; // result is false
```

Explanation: Here, result is `false` because the NOT operator flips `true` to `false`.

Combining Logical Operators

You can also combine these operators to create more complex conditions:

```
const x = 5;

const y = 10;

const isGreater = (x > 3) && (y < 15); // isGreater is true

const isEither = (x < 3) || (y > 15); // isEither is false

const notTrue = !(x === 5); // notTrue is false
```

Explanation: In this example:

`isGreater is true` because both conditions are true.

`isEither is false` because neither condition is true.

`notTrue is false` because the expression `x === 5` is true, and the NOT operator inverts it.

These logical operators are fundamental in controlling the flow of your code, especially in conditional statements.

---

typeof Operator

The `typeof` operator in JavaScript is used to determine the type of a variable or an expression. It returns a string indicating the type. Here are some examples along with explanations:

Example 1: Basic Types

```
console.log(typeof "Hello, World!"); // "string"

console.log(typeof 42);              // "number"

console.log(typeof true);             // "boolean"

console.log(typeof undefined);        // "undefined"

console.log(typeof null);             // "object" (this is a
known quirk in JavaScript)
```

Explanation:

- `typeof "Hello, World!"` returns `"string"` because it's a string value.
- `typeof 42` returns `"number"` since 42 is a numeric value.
- `typeof true` returns `"boolean"` because it's a boolean value.
- `typeof undefined` returns `"undefined"` when a variable has been declared but not assigned a value.
- `typeof null` returns `"object"` due to a historical bug in JavaScript.

Example 2: Complex Types

```
console.log(typeof { name: "Alice", age: 30 }); // "object"

console.log(typeof [1, 2, 3]);                   //
"object" (arrays are also objects)

console.log(typeof function() {});                 // "function"

console.log(typeof new Date());                    // "object"
```

Explanation:

- `typeof { name: "Alice", age: 30 }` returns `"object"` because it's an object literal.
- `typeof [1, 2, 3]` returns `"object"` because arrays are technically objects in JavaScript.
- `typeof function() {}` returns `"function"` since functions are first-class objects.
- `typeof new Date()` returns `"object"` because a Date is also an object.

Example 3: Checking for Specific Types

```
let variable = "Hello";


if (typeof variable === "string") {

    console.log("It's a string!");

} else {

    console.log("It's not a string.");

}
```

Explanation: In this example, we check if `variable` is of type `"string"` using the `typeof` operator. If it is, we log "It's a string!". In this case the variable is `"Hello";` which is a string because it's letters so the console should log `It's a string!`

As you can see , the `typeof` operator is useful for type checking and debugging, allowing developers to understand the data types they are working with in their code.

Bitwise XOR Operator

The `^` operator is a bitwise XOR (exclusive OR) operator. It compares two numbers on a bit level (binary) and returns 1 when the bits are different and 0 when they are the same.

Example:

```
let num1 = 5;   // Binary: 101

let num2 = 3;   // Binary: 011

let result = num1 ^ num2; // XOR: 110 (6 in decimal)

console.log(result); // Output: 6
```

Explanation:

- 5 in binary is `101`
- 3 in binary is `011`
- XOR compares the bits:
  - 1 ^ 0 = 1
  - 0 ^ 1 = 1
  - 1 ^ 0 = 0
- So the result is `110` (which is 6 in decimal).

Bitwise XOR can be useful in programming for various tasks, like:

- Finding differences between numbers.
- Swapping values without a temporary variable.
- Creating checksums for data verification.

As you can see, there is an operator to represent virtually every mathematical or logical operation.

Statements

Statements are lines of code that instruct the browser to perform a specific task or function. They are essentially a sequence of operators, values, and expressions that are grouped together and meant to be interpreted in a specific order or fashion.

Here's an example of a statement:

```
let x, y, z;

x = 7;

y = 3;

z = x + y;
```

As you can see, the statement is used to instruct the browser on how to solve `Z = X + Y`, which, based on the instruction, should be `10`.

Expressions

An expression is an example of a *statement*, it is a combination of values, variables, and operators. Essentially, it is a sequence of calculations that lead to a unique value, like a number sentence such as `5 + 3` = the value of `8` or `2*3` = the value of `6`.

Examples of expressions include arithmetic operations (you may recall these from the ***operators section***) such as `+` addition, `-` subtraction, `*` multiplication, and `/` division, as well as `&&` logical and `==` comparison operations.

As you can see from the examples, the symbols used in each expression are the same as the JavaScript operators mentioned earlier.

Comments

The last fundamental I want to cover in this chapter is how to make comments. To inform others about the instructions of the JavaScript code, developers are able to write **Comments**.

The comments also give the observer info on the **semantics** or the meaning of the code. To indicate a single-line comment, a user inputs double slashes `//`. Also, any code that is between the slashes, / and / is treated as a comment also.

Lastly, a comment can also be used to stop a line of code from being executed, for testing purposes. Here's an example of comments in action:

Code Snippet A: `let x = 5;    // I will be executed`

Code Snippet B: `// x = 6;    I will NOT be executed`

As you can see from the example, **Code Snippet A** will be executed because the expression `let x = 5;` is included before the double slashes //. While **Code Snippet B** will <u>not be executed</u> because the expression `x = 6;` is not included before the double slashes.

Overall, JavaScript comments are pretty straightforward, and they are good to use when you need to provide information about what the code is being used for. Also, if you want to stop a line of code from being executed, so you can test the code.

Error Handling

This is a more intermediate JavaScript concept, but it is worth mentioning here. Even well-written programs can encounter unexpected issues during execution. JavaScript provides built-in mechanisms to gracefully handle these errors without crashing the entire application. Proper **Error Handling** not only helps in debugging,but also improves the user experience by preventing unexpected behavior.

While it may not be the very first thing you learn (like variables or functions), it becomes essential as soon as you start building more complex and interactive programs. In real-world JavaScript applications, especially those that interact with users, APIs, or the DOM, things *will* go wrong. Error handling gives you the tools to respond gracefully rather than letting your program crash or behave unpredictably.

`try,catch, finally`

The `try...catch` block allows developers to handle exceptions — that is, runtime errors that interrupt normal code execution. The `try` block contains code that might throw an error. If an error occurs, control is passed to the `catch` block. Optionally, a `finally` block can be included to run code regardless of whether an error occurred or not.

Here's an example below:

```
try {

  const data = JSON.parse('{"name":"Jane"}');

  console.log(data.name);

} catch (error) {

  console.error("Parsing error:", error);

} finally {

  console.log("Execution completed.");

}
```

In this example, if `JSON.parse` fails (for example, due to invalid syntax), the error will be caught and handled in the `catch` block, and the message in `finally` will always run.

Throwing Custom Errors

JavaScript also allows developers to throw their own errors using the `throw` statement. This is useful for flagging specific conditions in your application that you want to treat as exceptions.

Example:

```
function divide(a, b) {

  if (b === 0) {

    throw new Error("Division by zero is not allowed.");

  }
```

```
  return a / b;
}
try {
  console.log(divide(10, 0));
} catch (error) {
  console.error("Custom Error:", error.message);
}
```

Here, a custom error is thrown when attempting to divide by zero. This helps in identifying and addressing issues based on the logic of the application, not just system errors.

Understanding how to use `try, catch, finally`, and `throw` custom errors allows developers to build more reliable and maintainable applications. It also provides a structured way to detect and recover from runtime issues, ensuring smoother operation and easier debugging.

Last Thoughts

Hopefully, by now you have a solid understanding of the fundamentals of JavaScript code. As you can see, even at it's most basic level, with JavaScript you can do powerful things like create math equations that basically solve themselves. You can also dive into very detailed things like logical operations, and comparison operations,again showing how you can do Math with ease with JavaScript, very cool. Now let's move on to the next topic.

Chapter 4: Control Structures

Once you know how to write basic code, the next step is to make that code do something interesting. That means making decisions, responding to conditions, and repeating tasks, kind of like humans do in real life.

In this section, you'll explore **Control Structures**, which are the decision-makers and timekeepers of JavaScript. You'll learn how to tell your code:

- "If this happens, then do that."
- "Otherwise, do something else."
- "Do this over and over until I say stop."

We'll cover **Conditional statements** like `if`, `else`, and `switch`, as well as **Loops** like `for`, `while`, and `do...while`. These tools allow you to write smarter, more dynamic programs that can react to input and perform tasks multiple times without rewriting the same code.

You'll also learn about **Events**, which allow JavaScript to respond to real-time interactions like clicks, keypresses, or mouse movements. When combined with control structures, events make your websites come alive with interactivity.

Like I said in Chapter 3, these are also considered to be fundamental components of JavaScript coding, so taking the time to learn how to add these components to your code will be useful in your future programming endeavors.

My hope is that by the end of this section, you'll be thinking like a developer, mapping out logic, making decisions, and giving your code the ability to adapt and respond. Alright, let's dig into these concepts.

Conditional Statements

Conditional statements determine whether or not pieces of code can run, or if it is true or false. Essentially, you use them to execute code only if certain conditions are met. There are three main types of conditional statements:

`if` statements: where if a condition is true it is used to specify execution for a block of code.

else statements: where if the same condition is false, it specifies the execution of a block of code. Also, there are else if statements: this specifies a new test if the first condition is false.

Lastly, switch statements: is a type of conditional statement used to perform different actions based on different values of a single expression.

Here's a code snippet example demonstrating the if statement and else statement:

```
let num = 7;

if (num > 10) {
  console.log("The number is greater than 10.");
} else if (num > 5) {
  console.log("The number is greater than 5 but less than or equal
to 10.");
} else {
  console.log("The number is less than or equal to 5.");
}
```

The let num = 7 indicates that the variable num will be assigned a value of 7.

The if statement, if (num > 10) checks whether the value of the num variable is greater than 10. If the statement is true , then the text: ("The number is greater than 10.") will be displayed on the user's console.

Since num is actually 7, this condition is false, so the next statement else if (num > 5) will be executed instead.

If the statement is true for this piece of code, then the text: ("The number is greater than 5 but less than or equal to 10.") will be displayed on the user's console.

But if the answer is false, then else statement is executed; if the value of num is less than 5, then the console will instead log: ("The number is less than or equal to 5.")

As you can see, conditional statements are a significant part of JavaScript programming and are a great way to make the code more dynamic and responsive to user input or other changing conditions.

Here's another example demonstrating the `switch` statement in action:

```
let day = "Monday";

switch(day) {
  case "Monday":
    console.log("Start of the work week.");
    break;
  case "Friday":
    console.log("Almost the weekend!");
    break;
  default:
    console.log("Just another day.");
}
```

This part of the code, `let day = "Monday";` is used to declare a variable named `day` and assign the string value `"Monday"`.

Next part of the code:

```
switch(day) {
```

This is a `switch` statement that evaluates the value of `day`.

Next part of the code:

```
case "Monday":
    console.log("Start of the work week.");
    break;
```

If `day` is `"Monday"`, it runs `console.log("Start of the work week.")`, then `break` exits the switch block to prevent the execution of any other cases.

```
case "Friday":
```

```
    console.log("Almost the weekend!");

    break;
```

If `day` is `"Friday"`, it prints `"Almost the weekend!"` and exits.

```
  default:

    console.log("Just another day.");
```

If `day` doesn't match any of the listed cases, this `default` block runs, printing `"Just another day."` In this example: Since `day` is `"Monday"`, the output will be:

```
Start of the work week.
```

The `switch` statement is especially useful when you have many possible values to check and want to keep the code organized instead of writing multiple `if...else if` conditions.

Loops

In JavaScript, **Loops** are used to repeatedly execute a block of code as long as a specified condition is true. This allows you to automate repetitive tasks, iterate over data structures like arrays, or perform actions a set number of times. There are several types of loops in JavaScript:

1. `for` Loop

The `for` loop is commonly used when you know in advance how many times you want to iterate.

```
for (let i = 0; i < 5; i++) {

  console.log(i); // Output: 0, 1, 2, 3, 4

}
```

- **Initialization**: `let i = 0;` — This runs once at the start of the loop.
- **Condition**: `i < 5;` — The loop continues as long as this condition is true.
- **Increment/Update**: `i++` — This runs after each iteration.

2. `while` Loop

The `while` loop repeats as long as a specified condition is true.

```
let i = 0;

while (i < 5) {

  console.log(i);

  i++;

}
```

---

3. `do...while` Loop

The `do...while` loop is similar to the `while` loop, but it ensures that the loop runs at least once, even if the condition is initially false.

```
let i = 0;

do {

  console.log(i);

  i++;

} while (i < 5);
```

---

4. `for...of` Loop

This loop iterates over iterable objects like arrays, strings, or sets.

```
let array = [10, 20, 30];

for (let value of array) {

  console.log(value); // Output: 10, 20, 30

}
```

5. `for...in` Loop

This loop iterates over the keys of an object or an array's indices.

```
let obj = { a: 1, b: 2, c: 3 };

for (let key in obj) {

  console.log(key); // Output: a, b, c

}
```

As you can see, Loops help make your code cleaner, more efficient, and easier to manage, especially when dealing with dynamic or large sets of information. Whether you're working with a `for` loop, a `while` loop, or a `for...of` loop, understanding how and when to use them gives you the power to automate and streamline your logic with precision and control.

Events

An **Event** is a signal or alert that is triggered when users interact with an HTML element on a webpage. Essentially, events are actions or occurrences that happen in the browser, like clicking a button, hovering over a link, or submitting a form. JavaScript allows you to "listen" for these events and respond to them.

Here's an example of an HTML code snippet that just uses the event `click`, which tells the browser to trigger an event when a button `<button>` is clicked on:

```
<button onclick="displayDate()">The time is?</button>
```

This particular event instructs the browser to display a date when the `button` is clicked on. As you can see, Events are a great way to build interactive web pages. Here are some other examples of JavaScript events.

Here are some common examples of JavaScript events:

- `mouseover` – occurs when the mouse pointer hovers over an element.
- `mouseout` – fired when the mouse pointer leaves an element.

- `keydown` – triggered when a user presses a key on the keyboard.
- `keyup` – fired when a key is released.
- `submit` – occurs when a form is submitted.
- `change` – triggered when the value of an input element changes.
- `load` – fired when the entire page or an image has finished loading.
- `resize` – occurs when the browser window is resized.
- `scroll` – triggered when a user scrolls within an element or page.

These events allow developers to create dynamic, interactive web experiences by responding to user actions in real time. By understanding how to handle these events, you can build applications that feel intuitive and responsive.

Last Thoughts

In this section, you've learned how to make your JavaScript programs more dynamic and responsive through conditional statements, loops, and events. Conditional statements allow your code to make decisions based on logic and user input, helping you control the flow of your program.

Loops are powerful tools that help you repeat tasks efficiently without writing repetitive code. And with events, you've gained the ability to make your web pages interactive, responding to user actions like clicks, keystrokes, and form submissions. Together, these components form the backbone of dynamic programming and bring your websites to life.

Chapter 5: Functions and Execution

Let's take a look at another essential JavaScript concept. In programming, we don't just store data, we *do things* with it. That's where **Functions** come in.

A function is a reusable block of code that performs a specific task. Whether it's calculating a score, formatting a string, or interacting with the page, functions allow you to group logic together and reuse it throughout your code.

But understanding functions in JavaScript goes deeper than just calling and writing them. You'll explore:

- How functions are declared and expressed
- What happens under the hood when a function runs (hint: it involves the **Call stack**!)
- How **Recursion** lets a function call itself, and when that's actually useful
- The nuances of `this`, **Scope**, and **Hoisting** in function contexts
- The magic of **Closures**, which allow functions to "remember" data even after they've finished running

This section lays the groundwork for understanding how *JavaScript actually runs* your code. If you've ever wondered why some things seem to happen out of order or why variables disappear or reappear, this section will bring clarity.

By the end, you won't just write functions, you'll understand how they think.

Functions

Let's discuss **Functions** in more detail. Functions are a code snippet that includes "procedures" or a set of statements and expressions that are grouped together for a specific purpose or to perform a task. Essentially, they are meant to be used over and over again as opposed to creating a new function for every use.

Here's an example:

```
function toCelsius(fahrenheit) {
  return (5/9) * (fahrenheit-32);
}
```

```
document.getElementById("demo").innerHTML = toCelsius(77);
```

The function includes several key parts:

```
function toCelsius(fahrenheit)
```

This statement identifies the function or procedure to be completed; in this case, the procedure is to convert Fahrenheit to Celsius.

Next part of the code snippet:

```
{
  return (5/9) * (fahrenheit-32);
}
```

This statement indicates the sequence of expressions to be completed in order to `return` the answer to the question.

Essentially, the statement is saying that to convert a Fahrenheit measurement to Celsius, the following steps must first be completed: Divide `5/9`, and take the inputted Fahrenheit measurement minus `- 32`. Then take the result of these two expressions and multiply * them. As you can see, the order in which these operations are performed is important in order to return the correct answer.

Then the last statement:

```
document.getElementById("demo").innerHTML = toCelsius(77);
```

Is instructing the computer to show the answer to the function on the user's screen via HTML, more specifically as an HTML tag with the `id "demo"` (Refer back to the *DOM (Dynamic Object Model)* manipulation section in Chapter 2).

The last part of the statement `toCelsius(77);` between the parentheses `()` is where the programmer would input the Fahrenheit number they wish to be converted.

In this case, the Fahrenheit number inputted was 77F. So the result should be 25C.

Again, functions are great because they allow you to write reusable pieces of code. Instead of repeating yourself, you define a function and use it multiple times throughout your program.

Call Stack

A **Call Stack** is a mechanism that keeps track of function calls in the order they need to be executed. To recall, a *Function* in JavaScript is a code snippet that includes "procedures" or a set of statements and expressions that are grouped together for a specific purpose or to perform a task. Think of a call stack as a stack of plates. When a function is invoked, it is placed on top of the stack.

Once that function finishes execution, it is removed from the stack, and the program continues with the next item below it. The call stack is not a list of functions waiting to be executed — it's a record of the functions that are currently being executed, in the order they were called. So essentially, it is a snapshot of or live view of what functions are currently being executing and what's waiting to finish. Once a function is done, it disappears from the call stack.

Let me provide a bit more clarity and detail by expanding on the "stack of plates" example I just gave earlier:

- When a function is called, it is added (or *pushed*) onto the top of the call stack.
- JavaScript **executes that function immediately**.
- If that function calls another function, the new function is pushed onto the stack.
- Once a function **completes**, it is removed (or *popped*) from the stack.
- Execution then returns to the previous function on the stack.

So, you might think of a call stack as a to-do list, but really the call stack is more like a **"what's happening now"** snapshot of nested function executions. It grows deeper as new functions are called and shrinks as they return.

The call stack operates in a **Last In, First Out (LIFO)** manner. This means the last function added to the stack is the first one to be executed and removed. If a function calls another function, the called function is added to the top of the stack and must complete before the program can return to the previous one.

```
function David() {
        Sam();
      }

function Sam() {
        Rick1();
        Rick2();
      }
function Rick1() {
        console.log("Who's name was called last");
      }
function Rick2() {
        console.log("Rick");
      }
David ();
```

What the Code Means:

1. `David() is called`
2. Inside `David()`, `Sam() is called`
3. Inside `Sam()`, `Rick1() is called`
4. `Rick1()` logs: `"Who's name was called last" →`
5. Next in `Sam()`, `Rick2() is called`
6. `Rick2()` logs: `"Rick" →`

7. Stack unwinds as `Sam()` and then `David()` return
8. The Console will then log `Who's name was called last` and `Rick`

Each function returned in reverse order (LIFO — Last In, First Out), and the stack unwound until it was empty. So again, the call stack shows what's currently being executed, not what's scheduled to run in the future. Below is another, more detailed example:

Example:

```
function greet() {

  console.log("Hello");

  askName();

}

function askName() {

  console.log("What is your name?");

}

greet();
```

Call Stack Flow:

- `greet()` is added to the stack.
- Inside `greet(), console.log("Hello")` is executed.
- `askName()` is called and added to the top of the stack.
- Inside `askName(), console.log("What is your name?")` is executed.
- `askName()` completes and is removed.
- `greet()` completes and is removed.

This linear flow of pushing and popping functions off the stack is how JavaScript keeps track of where it is in the code at all times. So, as you can see, the call stack is a great way to know what functions are executing and which ones are currently finishing up.

Recursion

Recursive functions are a commonality in JavaScript code; essentially, "**recursion**" means writing a function that calls itself inside its own "body" to solve a problem by breaking it down into smaller pieces. It's like asking for help repeatedly until the problem is easy enough to solve. Here's how it works: imagine you have a big stack of books to count. Instead of counting all at once, you say:

- "I'll count one book, then ask my friend to count the rest."
- Your friend does the same: counts one book, asks the next friend.
- This keeps happening until someone has just one book, then they say "1."
- Then everyone adds their counts as it goes back up the chain.

In code, it looks like this:

```
function countBooks(n) {
  if (n === 1) return 1;           // Base case: only one book left
  return 1 + countBooks(n - 1); // Count one book and ask to count
the rest
}
console.log(countBooks(5)); // Outputs 5
```

This is a good example of a recursive function because the function solves a big problem (counting books) by breaking it down into smaller, similar problems (counting one book plus the rest), calling itself each time until it reaches the simplest case (just one book). That pattern—calling itself with a smaller input and stopping at a base case—is exactly what makes a function recursive.

Let me give you one more example. Here's a simple and relatable recursive function example to drive the point home. Check out the example below. The function below counts down from a number to zero, like a timer ticking down:

```
function countdown(n) {
  if (n < 0) {
```

```
    return; // Base case: stop when below zero
  }
  console.log(n);
  countdown(n - 1); // Recursive call with smaller number
}

countdown(5);
```

This function displays an example of recursion because it calls itself with a smaller number each time (`n - 1`). Stops when the number is less than zero (base case), and then prints the number each step, counting down like a timer.

Stack Overflow

Now that we talked about recursion, let's go back to **Call Stack** for a second, and talk about "**Stack Overflow**": you needed to learn recursion first, to really get this concept. It is imperative to mention that errors such as "*stack overflow*" can occur when too many functions are placed on the stack without being completed.

Essentially, the call stack exceeds its "*memory limit*"; it's similar to piling too many documents on your desk: eventually, you run out of space and can't do anything else. In code, this causes the program to crash due to too many function calls. This can happen when a program enters into *infinite recursion,* or if too many functions are called, or the same function continuously calls itself. This can create an endless *loop*, leading to a "stack overflow".

Example:

```
function recurse() {
  recurse();
}
recurse();
```

What Happens:

- `recurse() is called`
- Inside `recurse(), the function calls itself again recurse()` is added.
- This keeps happening with no stopping condition.
- Eventually, the JavaScript engine runs out of memory for the stack and throws a `RangeError: Maximum call stack size exceeded.`

This example shows **uncontrolled recursion**, when a function calls itself over and over with no way to stop, leading to a stack overflow. So, as you can see, stack overflow can be an issue for healthy code execution, unless care is taken to ensure that functions can be repeatedly called without running into an error. Recursion also relates to **Scope** and **Closures,** the next two concepts we are going to be exploring.

Scope

Scope refers to the area in which variables are accessible or visible. It determines which parts of the code can use or modify a variable. Essentially, scope means the variable is known to the program in that block or function. Understanding scope is important for writing predictable, maintainable code and avoiding variable conflicts. There are different types of scope we now need to explore.

Global vs Local Scope

A variable declared outside of any function or block has **Global Scope** and can be accessed from anywhere in the code. In contrast, a variable declared inside a function or block has **Local Scope** and is only accessible within that specific function or block. Here's a thorough and detailed example to wrap your head around.

Example:

```
let officeMessage = "This message is visible company-wide";

function meeting() {

  let roomNote = "This note is only for the meeting room";
```

```
  console.log(officeMessage); // Accessible

  console.log(roomNote);      // Accessible

}

meeting();

console.log(officeMessage);  // Accessible

console.log(roomNote);       // Error: roomNote is not defined
```

In this example, the variable `officeMessage` can be accessed from both inside and outside the function, while `roomNote` is only accessible inside the variable `meeting()`. So, essentially, the office message can be accessed outside and inside the meeting, but the room note can only be accessed at the meeting.

So metaphorically speaking, if you was to go to the "meeting" you would be aware of both, "the message", and "room note", but if your friend doesn't go the meeting, they will just have access to the office message, and not the room note, because the room note was only declared in the meeting.

Function Scope vs Block Scope

Traditionally, JavaScript used Function Scope, where variables declared with `var` are scoped to the function they are in, even if they're declared inside a block like an `if` or `for` statement. However, ES6's 2015 version introduced Block Scope with `let` and `const`, which restricts variable access to the nearest set of curly braces `{}`. Here's an example of function scope and block scope.

Example:

```
function testScope() {

  if (true) {

    var functionScoped = "I exist in the whole function";

    let blockScoped = "I only exist inside this block";

  }
```

```
  console.log(functionScoped); // Works
  console.log(blockScoped);    // Error: blockScoped is not defined
}
```

This is an example of function and block scope because it shows that `var` is function-scoped, meaning it's accessible anywhere inside the function, even outside the `if` block. In contrast, `let` is block-scoped, so it only exists inside the block where it's defined — accessing it outside causes an error.

Knowing the difference between global, local, function, and block scope helps prevent variable conflicts and bugs.

Hoisting

Hoisting refers to the behavior where variable and function declarations are moved to the top of their containing scope during the *compilation phase*, before any code is actually executed. This means that variables and functions can sometimes be referenced before they appear in the code, but with important limitations based on how they are declared.

Function declarations are fully "hoisted", so they can be called before they are defined in the code. However, variables declared with `var` are hoisted but initialized with `undefined`, while variables declared with `let` and `const` are hoisted in a way that they remain in a "temporal dead zone" until their actual declaration is reached. Accessing them before that point results in a runtime error.

Example:

```
console.log(a); // undefined
var a = 5;
greet(); // "Hello"
function greet() {
  console.log("Hello");
}
```

```
console.log(b); // ReferenceError: Cannot access 'b' before
initialization

let b = 10;
```

In this example, the `var` variable `a` is hoisted, so the code doesn't break, but it logs `undefined` because the assignment happens later. The `greet` function works as expected, because function declarations are hoisted entirely. The variable `b`, declared with `let`, causes a reference error because it's in the temporal dead zone until its line is reached. It's like having a reserved parking spot (the variable `b` is in scope), but the car (the value, `b = 10`) hasn't arrived yet — you can't park or use the spot until the car shows up (the variable `b` is initialized).

Hoisting is important to understand because it affects how and when variables and functions are available during execution. Misunderstanding it can lead to subtle bugs, especially in larger codebases or when mixing different types of declarations.

Closures

A **Closure** is created when a function is defined inside another function and remembers the variables from the outer function, even after the outer function has finished executing. This allows the inner function to access and use variables from the outer scope. Here's a real-world-style closure example involving a login system, something most people are familiar with.

Example: Login Attempt Tracker

```
function createLogin(username) {

  let attempts = 0;

  return function(password) {

    attempts++;

    if (password === "secret123") {

      console.log(`Welcome, ${username}!`);

    } else {
```

```
      console.log(`Incorrect password. Attempt #${attempts}`);
    }
  };
}

const userLogin = createLogin("Jessica");

userLogin("guess1");     // Incorrect password. Attempt #1
userLogin("hello");      // Incorrect password. Attempt #2
userLogin("secret123"); // Welcome, Jessica!
```

This is an example of closure because the inner function remembers both the `username` and the `attempts` count, even after `createLogin` has finished running. Also, each time you call `userLogin`, it has access to those remembered variables. Lastly, no one outside can directly change `attempts` — it's safely "closed in."

So, essentially, running the function is like a login box that tracks how many times you try to log in, but only that box knows the counter. You can't see or change the count yourself — only the login box (closure) can.

To summarize, closures allow inner functions to retain access to variables from outer functions, even after those outer functions have finished executing, making them essential for managing private data and creating more flexible, stateful functions.

The `this` Keyword

The value of the `this` keyword depends entirely on the context in which a function is called. Unlike some programming languages, where this always refers to the current object, with JavaScript the `this` keyword is more dynamic and can change depending on how and where the function is invoked. Let's look at **Global Context, Object Method Context**, **Arrow Functions**, and **Event Handlers**.

Global Context

When used in the global scope (outside of any object or function, again refer back to that section for greater clarity), the keyword `this` refers to the global object—window in browsers or `global` in Node.js. If you didn't know, Node.js is a runtime that lets you run JavaScript on the server outside the browser. Let's look at an example of the `this` keyword in Global Context. Check it out below.

```
console.log(this); // In a browser, this refers to the window
object
```

`this` in the global scope points to the global object (`window` in browsers), representing the global context.

Object Method Context

When a function is called as a method of an object, `this` refers to the object that the method belongs to.

```
const person = {

  name: "Amber",

  greet() {

    console.log(`Hi, I'm ${this.name}`);

  },

};

person.greet(); // Hi, I'm Amber
```

Here, the variable `this.name` refers to the name property of the person object, because `greet()` was called as a method of that object.

Arrow Functions

Arrow functions behave differently, as in, they do not have their own `this`. Instead, they inherit `this` from their surrounding (lexical) scope. Look at the example below:

```
const user = {

  name: "Bob",
```

```
  greet: () => {
    console.log(`Hi, I'm ${this.name}`);
  },
};
user.greet(); // Hi, I'm undefined
```

In this example, the arrow function does not bind its own `this`, so it looks to the outer context (which is the global object), and `this.name` ends up being `undefined`.

Event Handlers

In event listeners, `this` refers to the DOM element that fired the event. Check out the example below:

```
document.querySelector("button").addEventListener("click", function () {
  console.log(this); // Logs the button element
});
```

However, if you use an arrow function, `this` will refer to the outer context, not the button.

Controlling `this`: `.call()`, `.apply()`, and `.bind()`

JavaScript provides three methods to explicitly control what `this` refers to in a function:

- `.call(thisArg, arg1, arg2, ...)` – Calls the function with a given `this` value and arguments passed individually.
- `.apply(thisArg, [args])` – Similar to `.call()`, but arguments are passed as an array.
- `.bind(thisArg)` – Returns a new function with this bound to the given value.

Here's an example

```
function sayHi() {
  console.log(`Hi, I'm ${this.name}`);
```

```
}

const person = { name: "Charlie" };


sayHi.call(person);  // Hi, I'm Charlie

sayHi.apply(person); // Hi, I'm Charlie


const boundHi = sayHi.bind(person);

boundHi();           // Hi, I'm Charlie
```

These tools are especially helpful when working with callbacks or event handlers where the value of this might otherwise be lost.

Last Thoughts

As you can see, functions are more than just tools to avoid repeating code, they're the heartbeat of JavaScript logic. By learning how to declare, call, and nest functions, you've gained the power to organize your code into clean, manageable pieces. You've also explored deeper concepts like scope, hoisting, closures, and recursion, ideas that are key to mastering how JavaScript truly works behind the scenes.

With this knowledge, you're not just writing functions, you're thinking like a JavaScript developer. Keep practicing, and soon these foundational concepts will become second nature as you build more advanced and interactive applications.

Chapter 6: Types and Typing Systems

JavaScript is famously "loosely typed," but that doesn't mean it doesn't care about types, it just handles them in ways that can be both flexible and surprising. If you've ever seen JavaScript turn a number into a string without you asking, or compared two values that *look* different but still returned `true`, then you've already encountered **JavaScript's type system** in action.

This section explores how JavaScript works with types behind the scenes. We'll cover the different ways JavaScript manages type checking and coercion, and how various typing philosophies, like **Implicit (Type Coercion)**, **Explicit typing, Nominal typing**, **Structural typing**, and **Duck typing**, can shape your thinking as a developer, even if JavaScript itself doesn't enforce strict rules. By the end of this section, you'll better understand JavaScript's quirky but powerful relationship with types, and how to write cleaner, more predictable code by anticipating how the language interprets your values.

Implicit (Type Coercion)

Type Coercion refers to JavaScript's automatic or implicit conversion of values from one data type to another. Because JavaScript is a loosely typed or dynamically typed language, variables are not bound to a specific type, and the interpreter frequently converts between types as needed, especially during operations like comparisons, arithmetic, or string concatenation. There are two types of Type Coercion.

Implicit Coercion

This occurs when JavaScript automatically converts a value from one type to another without being explicitly told to do so.

For example:

```
'5' + 1
```

In this case, the number `1` is implicitly converted into a string, so the result is the string `"51"` due to string concatenation.

```
'5' - 1
```

Here, the string `'5'` is implicitly converted to the number 5, and the subtraction operation results in the number `4`.

Implicit coercion can be convenient, but it may also produce unexpected results if you're not careful.

Explicit Coercion

This is when the developer intentionally converts a value to a different type using functions like `Number()`, `String()`, or `Boolean()`.

Examples:

```
Number("5") // returns 5 (string "5" becomes number 5)

String(10)  // returns "10" (number 10 becomes string "10")

Boolean(0)  // returns false (0 is falsy, so it's converted to
false)
```

Explicit coercion is generally preferred for clarity and predictability.

Common Coercion Rules

There are also some common rules that go with Type coercion worth noting as well:

Converting to a Number

JavaScript will **automatically convert other types into numbers** when it encounters operations that require numbers (like subtraction, multiplication, division, or when using the unary + operator).

- `"42"` becomes `42` because it's a numeric string.
- `true` becomes `1` and `false` becomes `0` because of their Boolean-to-number mapping.
- `null` becomes `0`.
- `undefined` becomes `NaN` (Not a Number), because it has no meaningful numeric equivalent.

Converting to a String

JavaScript will **coerce values to strings** when it encounters string operations like concatenation using the `+` operator (where at least one operand is a string), or when a string context is expected (like setting an HTML element's `.textContent`).

- A number like `5` becomes `"5"`.
- `null` becomes `"null"`.
- `undefined` becomes `"undefined"`.
- An array like `[1, 2]` becomes `"1,2"` as the array is converted to a comma-separated string of its elements.

Converting to a Boolean

JavaScript defines certain values as "falsy." These are: `0`, `""` (an empty string), `null`, `undefined`, `NaN`, and of course, `false`. All other values are considered "truthy," meaning they will evaluate to `true` in a Boolean context.

For instance:

```
Boolean(0)          // false (0 is falsy)

Boolean("hello")    // true (non-empty string is truthy)
```

Equality Comparisons: `==` vs. `===`

JavaScript has two types of equality operators: `==` (loose equality) and `===` (strict equality). The `==` operator performs type coercion if the two values being compared are of different types. In contrast, `===` does not perform any type coercion; it checks both value and type.

Examples:

```
0 == '0'          // true, because '0' is coerced to number 0

0 === '0'         // false, because number and string are different
types
```

```
null == undefined // true, because they are considered equal in loose comparison

null === undefined // false, because the types differ
```

This behavior can be confusing, which is why many developers recommend always using `===` to avoid unintended coercion.

Type coercion in JavaScript is the automatic or manual process of converting values from one data type to another. It comes in two forms: implicit coercion, where the JavaScript engine performs conversions automatically (for example, adding a string and a number results in a string), and explicit coercion, where the developer intentionally changes the type using built-in functions like `String()`, `Number()`, or `Boolean()`. While coercion can make JavaScript flexible, it also introduces potential for bugs, especially in equality comparisons using ==, which allows coercion, as opposed to ===, which does not. Understanding how and when coercion happens is essential for writing predictable and bug-free JavaScript code.

Explicit Typing

Explicit typing means the programmer directly defines what type a variable should be, like saying, “this must be a number” or “this must be a string.” This is common in statically typed languages like TypeScript, Java, or C#. JavaScript by itself does not have explicit typing because it is dynamically typed; it infers types as the code runs.

JavaScript lets you do this:

```
let age = 30;

age = "thirty"; // No error, now it's a string
```

JavaScript does not enforce types at all, so it won’t stop you from reassigning `age` to a string. However, you **can** use TypeScript (a typed layer over JavaScript) to add explicit typing.

Nominal Typing

Nominal typing or Nominal structuring means types are considered the same only if they were declared under the same name or structure definition. Even if two objects have identical properties, if they come from different types (with different names), the language treats them as incompatible unless explicitly cast or converted. JavaScript does not use nominal typing. You can create two objects with similar structures and use them interchangeably, as long as the data matches what's expected.

```
let person = { name: "Stacy" };

let employee = { name: "Craig" };


// You can pass either object into a function that expects an object with a 'name' property.

function greet(obj) {

    console.log("Hello, " + obj.name);

}


greet(person);   // "Hello, Stacy"

greet(employee); // "Hello, Craig"
```

The example shows that JavaScript is not nominally typed because it allows objects like `person` and `employee`, which have the same structure but no formal type relationship—to be used interchangeably. In nominal typing (used in languages like Java or C#), two objects must come from the same explicitly named type to be considered compatible, even if they have the same properties. JavaScript instead uses **structural typing** and **duck typing**, meaning it checks whether an object has the necessary properties (like `name`) rather than caring about its declared type name. We will explore both of those terms next.

Structural Typing

Structural typing checks whether a value fits the required shape. If it does, it's considered valid, even if it wasn't created from a named type. In JavaScript, there are no types at all, but this kind of flexibility is exactly how JavaScript works. If a function needs a property, JavaScript doesn't care what the object is called, just that the property exists. Check out the example below:

```
function greet(person) {
    console.log("Hi, " + person.name);
}

let anotherUser = { name: "Fred", role: "admin" };
greet(anotherUser); // "Hi, Fred"
```

This example demonstrates **structural typing** because the function `greet` accepts any object that has a `name` property, regardless of what other properties it has or where it came from. The object `anotherUser` has extra properties like `role`, but since it matches the required structure by including a `name` field, it is accepted and works correctly. This shows that compatibility is based on an object's shape, not its explicit type or origin, which is the core idea of structural typing.

Duck Typing

Duck typing is an informal form of structural typing, "If it walks like a duck and quacks like a duck, it's a duck." That means an object is valid if it has the necessary behavior (properties or methods), regardless of where it came from.

Example in JavaScript:

```
function drive(vehicle) {
    if (vehicle.startEngine) {
        vehicle.startEngine();
    }
}

let car = {
```

```
    startEngine: function() {
        console.log("Engine started");
    }
};

drive(car); // "Engine started"
```

Here, the `drive` function doesn't care if `car` is actually from a `Car` class. As long as the object has a `startEngine` method, it's treated like a valid vehicle. Duck typing is what makes JavaScript so dynamic; you can pass in objects with the right methods or properties, and the function will work, even without a defined class or type.

Last Thoughts

To wrap up this chapter, you've now gained a solid understanding of how JavaScript handles types, an often tricky but essential part of mastering the language. We explored how JavaScript's flexible type system, with its implicit coercion and unique typing philosophies, affects the way your code behaves.

This knowledge equips you to anticipate and avoid common pitfalls, helping you write cleaner, more predictable programs. As you move forward, keeping these type concepts in mind will make your JavaScript coding smoother and more effective, setting a strong foundation for the more advanced topics ahead.

Chapter 7: Objects and Collections

Objects are at the heart of JavaScript. Whether you're working with a simple data structure, interacting with the DOM, or creating complex applications, you're almost always dealing with objects in one form or another. JavaScript uses objects not just to store key-value pairs, but also to define most of its fundamental structures: including arrays, functions, and even the `Math` library.

This section starts with the basics, what objects are and how they work, before introducing you to collections like `Map`, `Set`, `WeakMap`, and `WeakSet`. These modern data structures solve real-world problems like avoiding accidental key collisions or improving memory efficiency by allowing garbage collection.

By the end of this section, you'll have a clear understanding of how to use objects effectively, when to reach for newer collections, and how to choose the right tool for your data-handling needs.

Objects and Collections

To recall from Chapter 2, **Objects** are a fundamental type used to store collections of data as key-value pairs. Think of an object as a simple collection where each key (also called a property) is a unique identifier linked to a value, which can be anything—numbers, strings, functions, or even other objects. This makes objects incredibly flexible for organizing and managing related pieces of information together.

JavaScript also offers some powerful built-in **collection types** to store and manage groups of data beyond plain arrays and objects. The most common ones are:

Map

A `Map` stores key-value pairs, just like a regular object, but with more flexibility; keys can be any data type. Think of it as a supercharged object. It stores key-value pairs, but unlike regular objects, keys can be *any* type: objects, functions, or primitives. Maps also remember the order of *insertion*, insertion simply means adding something into a specific place. In programming, when we talk about insertion, like in the context of a `Map` or an array, it means adding a new item or entry into that data structure. Let's check out an example below.

Example:

```
const userRoles = new Map();
```

```
userRoles.set('sarah', 'admin');
userRoles.set('tom', 'editor');
userRoles.set(123, 'guest');  // Number as a key!

console.log(userRoles.get('sarah')); // Output: admin
console.log(userRoles.get(123));     // Output: guest

// Iterate over entries
for (const [user, role] of userRoles) {
  console.log(`${user}: ${role}`);
}
```

Let's break down why this is a good example of the `Map` object. First, it allows any data type as a key, like the number `123`, which wouldn't behave reliably as a key in a regular object. Second, it maintains *insertion order*, so when you iterate over `userRoles`, entries come out in the order they were added. Finally, using `set()` and `get()` makes the syntax clear and intentional. This example clearly demonstrates `Map`'s strengths: flexible keys, predictable iteration, and efficient key-value pairing.

WeakMap

A `WeakMap` is a special kind of map where: Keys must be objects (not strings, numbers, etc.). It holds a *weak* reference to the keys, meaning if the object is no longer used elsewhere in your program, it can be garbage collected. You can't loop through a `WeakMap`, and it doesn't have a `.size` property. It's useful when you want to attach data to an object without preventing it from being cleaned up when you're done with it.

Example:

```
const button = document.querySelector('button');
const buttonData = new WeakMap();
```

```
// Store some data about the button
buttonData.set(button, { clicks: 0 });

button.addEventListener('click', () => {
  let data = buttonData.get(button);
  data.clicks++;
  console.log(`Clicked ${data.clicks} times`);
});
```

Here, the `button` element is the key, and the WeakMap stores metadata (`{ clicks: 0 }`) about it. When the button is clicked, the code safely updates and logs the click count using the WeakMap. If the `button` gets removed from the page and nothing else refers to it, the data in `WeakMap` gets cleaned up automatically. Since WeakMaps hold weak references to keys, if the button element is removed from the DOM (Document Object Model) and no other references exist, it can be garbage collected, preventing memory leaks.

Set

A `Set` is like an array, but it only stores *unique* values. No duplicates allowed. A `Set` stores unique values. If you add the same value twice, it only keeps one. This is handy when you want to filter out repeated data easily. `Set` helps you quickly remove duplicates or test if something exists without looping.

Example:

```
const numbers = new Set();

numbers.add(1);
numbers.add(2);
numbers.add(2);  // Duplicate ignored
```

```
console.log(numbers.has(1)); // true
console.log(numbers.size);   // 2

// Loop through the Set
for (const num of numbers) {
  console.log(num);
}
```

This example clearly shows how a `Set` works in JavaScript because it highlights its key feature: uniqueness of values. When you add numbers `1` and `2`, they get stored in the `Set`. But when you try to add `2` again, the `Set` ignores the duplicate, so the size remains `2`. Using `numbers.has(1)` demonstrates how Sets let you quickly check if a value exists, and `numbers.size` tells you how many unique items are inside. The loop shows how you can easily *iterate*, or go through each item in a collection—like an array, object, Map, or Set—one by one, usually to perform some action on each item. Overall, this example perfectly illustrates how Sets store only unique elements and provide efficient membership checks.

WeakSet

A `WeakSet` is similar to a regular `Set`, but it only stores objects, not primitive data types. It also holds *weak references*, so objects can be garbage collected. You can't iterate over a `WeakSet`, and you won't know how many items it has. Use `WeakSet` when you want to *remember if you've seen an object* without stopping it from being cleaned up.

Example:

```
const onlineUsers = new WeakSet();

const user1 = { name: 'Pam' };
const user2 = { name: 'Phil' };
```

```
onlineUsers.add(user1);

console.log(onlineUsers.has(user1)); // true
console.log(onlineUsers.has(user2)); // false

// Later...
user1 = null; // If nothing else references this user, it will be
cleaned up
```

This example is a solid demonstration of how a `WeakSet` works because it shows the key feature of WeakSets: they store objects weakly, meaning they don't prevent those objects from being garbage collected if there are no other references. Here, `onlineUsers` tracks which user objects are "online." Adding `user1` puts that object into the `WeakSet`, so `onlineUsers.has(user1)` returns `true`. Since `user2` was never added, it returns `false`. When `user1` is set to `null` and no other references exist, it can be cleaned up by JavaScript's memory management, which wouldn't be possible with a regular `Set`.

Last Thoughts

To wrap up this section, you now have a strong grasp of why objects are fundamental to JavaScript and how they form the backbone of everything from simple data storage to complex application logic. You've explored not only the basics of objects but also advanced collections like Map, Set, WeakMap, and WeakSet, understanding their unique benefits and practical use cases.

With this knowledge, you're well-equipped to manage data more efficiently, avoid common pitfalls, and choose the right structures to build robust, maintainable code. As you continue your journey, these concepts will be key tools in your JavaScript toolkit, empowering you to handle data with confidence and precision.

Chapter 8: Modern JavaScript Features

Like I said, JavaScript is always evolving. Over the years, new features have been added to the language that make writing code more expressive, concise, and powerful. In this section, we'll explore some of the most popular modern features like **Destructuring**, **Spread/Rest Operators**, **JSON Handling**, and **Modules**. These tools help you write cleaner code, manage data more efficiently, and organize your projects with better modularity.

Destructuring and Spread/Rest Operators

JavaScript provides convenient syntax for working with arrays and objects through **Destructuring** and the **Spread/Rest Operators**. These features help write cleaner and more readable code by making it easier to extract, copy, and combine data.

Destructuring

Destructuring allows you to extract values from objects or arrays and assign them to variables in a single, concise statement. This avoids repetitive code and makes variable assignment straightforward.

Example (Object Destructuring):

```
const user = { name: "Tiffany", age: 22 };

const { name, age } = user;


console.log(name); // Tiffany

console.log(age);  // 22
```

Here, the properties `name` and `age` from the user object are extracted and stored in variables with the same names.

Spread Operator (`...`)

The spread operator lets you expand elements of an array or properties of an object. It's commonly used to copy arrays or objects, or merge them without modifying the original.

Example (Array Spread):

```
const arr1 = [1, 2, 3];

const arr2 = [...arr1, 4, 5];


console.log(arr2); // [1, 2, 3, 4, 5]
```

In the array spread example, `const arr2 = [...arr1, 4, 5];` uses the spread syntax (`...arr1`) to copy all elements from `arr1` into a new array, and then adds `4` and `5` at the end. The result is `[1, 2, 3, 4, 5]`. This is useful for combining or cloning arrays without modifying the original.

Example (Object Spread):

```
const obj1 = { x: 1, y: 2 };

const obj2 = { ...obj1, z: 3 };


console.log(obj2); // { x: 1, y: 2, z: 3 }
```

In the object spread example, `const obj2 = { ...obj1, z: 3 };` copies all key-value pairs from `obj1` into a new object, then adds a new property `z: 3`. The result is `{ x: 1, y: 2, z: 3 }`. Object spread is commonly used to merge or extend objects while keeping the original unchanged.

Rest Operator `(...)`

The rest operator uses the same syntax (`...`) but serves the opposite purpose: it collects multiple elements into a single array or object. It is often used in function parameters to handle an arbitrary number of arguments.

Example:

```
function sum(...numbers) {

  return numbers.reduce((total, num) => total + num, 0);

}
```

```
console.log(sum(1, 2, 3, 4)); // 10
```

Here, `...numbers` gathers all arguments passed into the function into an array called `numbers`. This is a great example of the rest operator in action because it shows how you can collect an unknown number of arguments into a single array-like variable. In the function `sum(...numbers)`, the `...numbers` syntax uses the rest operator to gather all the arguments passed to `sum()` into one array called `numbers`. This allows the function to work with any number of values, not just a fixed amount. Then, `reduce` adds them all together. It's a clear, flexible example showing how the rest operator helps handle variable numbers of inputs cleanly and concisely.

Understanding destructuring and spread/rest operators is important because they simplify how you work with data structures, making your code cleaner, easier to read, and less error-prone.

JSON Handling

JSON stands for JavaScript Object Notation. It is a lightweight, text-based data format that is easy for humans to read and write, and easy for machines to parse and generate. JSON is widely used for data interchange, particularly in web applications where data needs to be sent between a server and a client.

`JSON.stringify()` and `JSON.parse()`

JavaScript provides two key methods for working with JSON: `JSON.stringify()` and `JSON.parse()`. These methods are used to convert JavaScript objects to JSON strings and back again.

Example:

```
const user = { name: "Pam", age: 30 };

const jsonString = JSON.stringify(user); // Converts object to JSON
string

console.log(jsonString); // Output: {"name":"Pam","age":50}
```

```
const parsedUser = JSON.parse(jsonString); // Converts JSON string back to object

console.log(parsedUser.name); // Output: Pam
```

`JSON.stringify()` is typically used when sending data to a server, while `JSON.parse()` is used to interpret JSON received from a server or external source.

Data Interchange Format for APIs

JSON has become the standard format for APIs (Application Programming Interface), which is a set of rules and protocols that allow different software programs to communicate and exchange data. Because JSON is language-independent, compact, and natively supported in JavaScript, it is the preferred choice for APIs. When making requests to or receiving responses from APIs, the payload is often formatted as JSON. This makes it easy to transport structured data, such as user profiles, configuration settings, or form inputs, between different systems.

Knowing how to use JSON effectively is crucial for any JavaScript developer, especially when working with APIs or storing and retrieving data. Its simplicity and compatibility with modern tools make it a fundamental component in building dynamic and connected web applications.

Modules

As JavaScript applications grow in size and complexity, managing code in a single file becomes increasingly difficult. To address this, JavaScript introduced **Modules**, which is a way to split code into separate files, each handling a specific responsibility. This makes code easier to maintain, test, and reuse across projects.

Import/export (ES6 Modules)

Modern JavaScript uses **ES6 modules**, which allow developers to explicitly export values (such as functions, objects, or variables) from one file and import them into another. This improves the structure of the codebase and reduces naming conflicts.

Here's an example:

math.js

```
export function add(a, b) {
```

```
  return a + b;
}
export const PI = 3.14159;
```

main.js

```
import { add, PI } from './math.js';

console.log(add(2, 3));  // Output: 5
console.log(PI);         // Output: 3.14159
```

This example clearly shows how JavaScript modules work by splitting code into separate files with `export` and `import`. In `math.js`, the `add` function and `PI` constant are exported, making them available outside the file. Then, in `main.js`, these exports are imported using `import { add, PI } from './math.js'`, allowing the code to use those functions and values directly. This modular approach helps organize code better, promotes reusability, and keeps files focused on specific tasks, which makes larger projects easier to manage.

As you can see, Modules encourage the separation of concerns, where each file or module focuses on a single piece of functionality, such as utility functions, data models, or API interactions. This modular design enhances code reusability, simplifies debugging, and makes collaborative development easier by enabling multiple developers to work on different parts of the application independently.

Last Thoughts

As you've seen in this section, modern JavaScript features aren't just about writing less code, they're about writing *better* code. Destructuring helps you unpack values neatly, the Spread and Rest operators give you flexibility when working with arrays and objects, JSON makes data exchange between systems seamless, and Modules bring structure and maintainability to your projects.

These features reflect the evolution of JavaScript into a more sophisticated, developer-friendly language. By embracing these tools, you're not just keeping up with the times, you're setting yourself up to write smarter, more efficient code in every project ahead.

Chapter 9: Asynchronous JavaScript

JavaScript runs on a single thread, which means it can only do one thing at a time. But modern apps require handling tasks like fetching data, reading files, or waiting for user input without freezing the interface. That's where **Asynchronous JavaScript** comes in. This section covers **Promises**, **Generators**, and **Async/Await**, powerful tools that let your code handle multiple operations smoothly and elegantly, improving the user experience and performance.

Promises

A **Promise** represents a value that may not be available yet but will be resolved in the future. It allows developers to write asynchronous code in a structured and manageable way. Essentially, it's like a *placeholder* for a result that isn't available yet but will be in the future, Promises let you write code that waits for that result without blocking everything else. A promise has three states: *pending*, *fulfilled*, or *rejected*.

Here is an extended example of pending, fulfilled, and rejected promises in JavaScript:

```
// Pending Promise: neither fulfilled nor rejected yet

let pendingPromise = new Promise((resolve, reject) => {

  // never calls resolve or reject, so stays pending

});


// Fulfilled Promise: operation completed successfully

let fulfilledPromise = new Promise((resolve, reject) => {

  resolve("Success!");

});

fulfilledPromise.then(value => console.log("Fulfilled with:",
value));
```

```
// Rejected Promise: operation failed

let rejectedPromise = new Promise((resolve, reject) => {

  reject("Error occurred!");

});

rejectedPromise.catch(error => console.log("Rejected with:",
error));
```

Here's why this is a good example that shows each promise state:

Pending Promise:

```
let pendingPromise = new Promise((resolve, reject) => {

  // never calls resolve or reject

});
```

This promise stays pending forever because neither `resolve` nor `reject` is called. It perfectly illustrates a promise that's still waiting on something to happen.

Fulfilled Promise:

```
let fulfilledPromise = new Promise((resolve, reject) => {

  resolve("Success!");

});
```

This promise calls `resolve` immediately, so it moves from pending to fulfilled state with a successful result (`"Success!"`). It clearly shows a promise that was completed successfully.

Rejected Promise:

```
let rejectedPromise = new Promise((resolve, reject) => {
```

```
    reject("Error occurred!");
  });
```

This promise calls `reject` immediately, so it moves from pending to rejected state with an error (`"Error occurred!"`). It demonstrates a promise that was finished but failed.

Together, these examples clearly illustrate how promises transition through their different states. I included another example below to help drive the point home.

Example:

```
fetch('https://api.example.com/data')
  .then(response => response.json())
  .then(data => console.log(data))
  .catch(error => console.error("Error:", error));
```

In this example, the `fetch()` call returns a Promise. If it succeeds, the `.then()` blocks are executed in sequence. If an error occurs, the `.catch()` block handles it. This chaining makes it easier to handle complex asynchronous flows. So again, as you can see, Promises are a great way to add more flexibility to your code.

Generators

Generators are a special kind of function that you can pause and resume, imagine a function with a "yield" button. They're functions that don't run all at once. Instead, they can yield multiple values over time and keep their state between yields. They're great for handling sequences of data, lazy evaluation (only producing values when needed), or managing asynchronous flows before async/await became widespread.

Example:

```
function* countUpTo(max) {
  let count = 1;
  while (count <= max) {
```

```
    yield count;  // Pause here and output count

    count++;

  }

}


const counter = countUpTo(3);


console.log(counter.next()); // { value: 1, done: false }

console.log(counter.next()); // { value: 2, done: false }

console.log(counter.next()); // { value: 3, done: false }

console.log(counter.next()); // { value: undefined, done: true }
```

This code defines a generator function `countUpTo(max)` that yields numbers from 1 up to the given maximum, pausing at each `yield`. When `countUpTo(3)` is called, it returns a generator object (`counter`) that doesn't run immediately. Each call to `counter.next()` resumes the function from where it left off, returning the next number and then pausing again. This behavior shows generators in action — they let you "wait for it" by pausing execution and returning control back to the caller until explicitly told to continue, creating a step-by-step flow of values.

You can think of a generator like a bookmark in a book, each time you call `counter.next()` , you read the next page and then pause again.

Async/Await

While `.then()` and `.catch()` work well, nested or chained promises can become difficult to read. **Async/Await** is a cleaner syntax built on top of Promises that allows asynchronous code to look and behave more like synchronous code.

Example:

```
async function loadData() {

  try {
```

```
        const response = await fetch('https://api.example.com/
data');
        const data = await response.json();
        console.log(data);
    } catch (error) {
        console.error("Error:", error);
    }
}
```

The `await` keyword pauses the execution of the function until the Promise is resolved, and the `async` keyword marks the function as asynchronous. This makes the code easier to write and reason about, especially when dealing with multiple asynchronous steps.

Last Thoughts

As you've now seen, asynchronous JavaScript is essential for building responsive, efficient applications. By understanding how Promises, Generators, and Async/Await work, you've gained the ability to write code that doesn't block the browser or frustrate users.

These tools allow you to manage time-consuming operations like data fetching, file reading, or delayed actions with clarity and control. With asynchronous techniques in your toolkit, you're now equipped to build modern apps that feel fast, fluid, and user-friendly, even when juggling multiple tasks at once.

Chapter 10: Practice Activities

Now that you've learned the basics of JavaScript, it's time to test your understanding with some hands-on practice. Practice is essential for mastering web development, and the more you experiment with JavaScript, the more you'll solidify the concepts you've learned.

In this chapter, we will present a series of exercises that focus on key JavaScript concepts like manipulating the DOM, handling events, working with variables, and controlling the flow of a program.

These exercises are designed to help you build interactive web pages with basic JavaScript functionality. By completing them, you'll gain confidence in applying your JavaScript knowledge to actual projects.

---

1. Displaying Text with JavaScript

Question: Create a simple webpage and use JavaScript to display text dynamically:

- A heading that says "Hello, JavaScript!" should appear when the page loads.
- Add a button that, when clicked, changes the heading to say "You clicked the button!"

Hint: Use `document.getElementById()` to select the heading and `addEventListener()` to trigger a function when the button is clicked.

---

2. Simple Math Operations

Question: Write a JavaScript program that performs basic math operations:

- Create two variables: one with the value 10 and another with the value 5.
- Display the result of adding, subtracting, multiplying, and dividing these numbers in the browser.

Hint: Use JavaScript arithmetic operators (+, -, *, /) and `console.log()` or `document.write()` to display the results.

---

3. Changing Element Style with JavaScript

Question: Create a webpage that allows users to change the style of an element:

- Add a paragraph of text that says, "Change my color!" and a button.
- When the button is clicked, change the text color to red.

Hint: Use `document.querySelector()` to select the paragraph and `style.color` to change its color.

---

4. Handling User Input

Question: Create a simple form and use JavaScript to handle the user input:

- Add a text input field and a button.
- When the user types something and clicks the button, display the typed text below the form.

Hint: Use `document.getElementById()` to get the value of the input field, and `innerHTML` to display the text on the page.

---

5. Building a Simple Counter

Question: Create a webpage with a simple counter:

- Add a button that says "Click Me!" and a paragraph that starts with "Clicks: 0".
- Each time the button is clicked, increment the counter and update the paragraph to show the new count.

Hint: Use a JavaScript variable to store the count, and update the text using `innerHTML` or `textContent`.

---

6. Basic Event Handling

Question: Set up event handlers to respond to user actions:

- Create a webpage with a button that says "Hover over me!".
- When the user hovers over the button, change its background color to green.
- When the mouse leaves the button, change the background color back to its original color.

Hint: Use `addEventListener()` for `mouseover` and `mouseout` events.

---

7. Simple To-Do List

Question: Build a basic to-do list using JavaScript:

- Add an input field and a button to allow the user to type in a task.
- When the user clicks the button, the task should be added as a list item below the input field.

Hint: Use `createElement()` to create new list items and `appendChild()` to add them to the page.

---

8. Creating a Random Number Generator

Question: Write a JavaScript program that generates random numbers:

- Add a button that says "Generate Random Number."
- When the button is clicked, display a random number between 1 and 100 on the page.

Hint: Use `Math.random()` and `Math.floor()` to generate the random number.

---

9. Basic Conditional Statements

Question: Create a webpage that responds to user input with a conditional statement:

- Add a text input field where the user can type their age.
- When the user clicks a button, display a message saying "You are old enough to drive!" if the age is 16 or older. Otherwise, display "You are not old enough to drive."

Hint: Use an `if-else` statement to compare the user's input.

---

10. Simple Loops

Question: Write a JavaScript program that uses a loop:

- Create a button that, when clicked, displays the numbers from 1 to 5 on the page.

Hint: Use a `for` loop to iterate through the numbers and `innerHTML` to display them on the page.

---

11. Change Background Color

Question: Make a button that changes the background color of the page.

- Each time the button is clicked, the background color should change to a new random color.

Hint: Use `Math.random()` to generate RGB values and `document.body.style.backgroundColor`.

---

12. Form Validation

Question: Validate a form before submission.

- Create a form that asks for a name and email. Prevent form submission if either field is empty or the email is invalid.

Hint: Use `addEventListener('submit', ...)` and `event.preventDefault()` to stop the form from submitting.

---

13. Toggle Light Bulb

Question: Create an interactive light bulb toggle.

- Use an image to represent a light bulb. Clicking a button should toggle the bulb on and off by switching the image source.

Hint: Use `getElementById()` and the `src` attribute of the image.

---

14. Character Counter

Question: Show a live character count for a textarea.

- As the user types in a textarea, display how many characters they've typed.

Hint: Use the `input` event and `value.length`.

---

15. Image Slider

Question: Create a simple image slider.

- Have multiple images that change every 2 seconds in a slideshow.

Hint: Use an array of image URLs and `setInterval()` to cycle through them.

---

16. Tip Calculator

Question: Create a tip calculator for a restaurant bill.

- Ask the user for the bill amount and the tip percentage, then calculate and display the tip and total amount.

Hint: Use `Number()` to convert inputs and basic arithmetic to calculate totals.

---

17. Guess the Number Game

Question: Make a number guessing game.

- The computer picks a random number between 1 and 100. The user has to guess the number, and the program gives hints (too high, too low) until the user gets it.

Hint: Use `Math.random()` and a `while` or `do...while` loop.

---

18. Rock, Paper, Scissors Game

Question: Build a simple rock-paper-scissors game.

- Let the user select Rock, Paper, or Scissors and compare it against a randomly generated computer choice.

Hint: Use `Math.random()` for the computer's choice and conditional statements to determine the winner.

---

19. Digital Clock

Question: Display the current time and update it every second.

- Create a digital clock that shows hours, minutes, and seconds.

Hint: Use `setInterval()` and `new Date()` to get the current time and update the DOM.

---

20. Accordion Menu

Question: Build an FAQ section with toggling answers.

- Clicking on a question reveals or hides its answer.

Hint: Use `addEventListener('click')` and `classList.toggle()` to show/hide content.

---

21. Word Counter Tool

Question: Count words in real time as the user types in a text area.

- Display the number of words typed below the text box.

  Hint: Split the string by spaces and filter out empty values.

---

22. Image Zoom on Hover

Question: Zoom in on an image when the mouse hovers over it.

- Add an effect that scales up the image slightly and returns it to normal when the mouse leaves.

Hint: Use `mouseover` and `mouseout` events and CSS transforms via JavaScript.

---

23. Keyboard Event Visualizer

Question: Show which key a user presses in real-time.

- Display the key code and key name whenever a key is pressed.

Hint: Use the `keydown` event and `event.key / event.code`.

---

24. Tabbed Content Interface

Question: Switch between different content sections by clicking tabs.

- Only one content section is visible at a time based on the active tab.

Hint: Loop through tabs and use `addEventListener()` and `classList` to toggle visibility.

---

25. Weather App (using a free API)

Question: Fetch and display real-time weather data.

- Enter a city name and display the current weather using a weather API (like OpenWeatherMap).

Hint: Use `fetch(), async/await`, and update the DOM with the API response.

Last Thoughts

These 25 practice activities are designed to cover a range of essential JavaScript skills, from basic DOM manipulation and event handling to user input and simple conditional logic. By working through these exercises, you will reinforce what you have learned and start applying JavaScript to real-world scenarios.

As you complete each task, review the output in your browser to ensure that the JavaScript behaves as expected. Remember: mastering JavaScript takes practice. The more you work through exercises like these, the more comfortable you'll become with writing interactive code, setting the foundation for more advanced topics like animations, AJAX, and JavaScript frameworks.

Chapter 11: Closing

Now that you've worked your way through the fundamentals and key concepts of JavaScript, take a moment to appreciate how far you've come. What started as curiosity about the language behind interactive websites has turned into a solid understanding of how JavaScript powers modern digital experiences. You've explored the essentials, from variables and loops to functions, objects, events, asynchronous logic, and even some of the powerful new features that make modern JavaScript so expressive and efficient.

You've learned about functions that run on command, created logic that responds to user actions, built data structures that store and organize information, and even handled unexpected behavior with error handling and conditionals. What was once mysterious is now manageable. You've taken the first big step toward becoming not just a passive consumer of the web, but an active creator.

The truth is, JavaScript doesn't just make things work; it makes things possible. It gives you the power to design, build, and control dynamic interfaces that users can interact with in real time. And beyond the browser, it opens doors to server-side development, mobile apps, APIs, and desktop tools.

Whether you're diving deeper into front-end development, enhancing your digital marketing strategies with technical insight, or planning a full transition into tech, JavaScript will be a powerful asset in your toolbox. Keep experimenting, keep building, and don't stop asking questions. The learning never ends, but that's what makes coding so exciting.

Remember: every expert developer once wrote their first `console.log("Hello, world!")`. What matters is consistency, curiosity, and creativity. You've got the foundation. Now take what you've learned, and start building the future you want, one script at a time.

Let this be the start, not the finish. The code is yours, go make something awesome with it. Before you leave, I want to give a few tips to help you as you continue your JavaScript journey.

Here are **5 solid tips** to help you keep growing and improving your JavaScript skills:

1. Build Real Projects (Even Small Ones Count)

Hands-on practice beats passive reading every time. Start with small projects like a calculator, quiz app, or countdown timer, then move on to more complex things like a weather app or task manager. Each project will teach you how to solve real problems and strengthen your understanding. So, definitely refer back to Chapter 10, for project ideas.

2. Read and Reverse-Engineer Other People's Code

Browse GitHub repositories, CodePen examples, or open-source projects. Read the code, try to understand it, and then tweak it. Ask yourself: *Why did they write it this way? What happens if I change this part?* Reverse-engineering teaches you patterns and better habits.

3. Break Stuff (On Purpose)

Don't be afraid to experiment and make mistakes. Intentionally break your code and try to fix it. It's one of the fastest ways to learn debugging, understand browser behavior, and discover how JavaScript really works under the hood.

4. Master the Fundamentals Before Jumping to Frameworks

It's tempting to rush into frameworks like React, Vue, or Angular, but strong knowledge of core JavaScript (variables, functions, DOM manipulation, events, async logic) is essential. Frameworks change, your JavaScript foundation should be rock-solid.

5. Practice Every Day, Even Just 15 Minutes

Consistency trumps cramming. Even if you're busy, spending a little time coding daily helps reinforce what you've learned. Use challenges from websites like freeCodeCamp, JavaScript30, or LeetCode to stay sharp.

Last Words

I hope these tips benefit you greatly as you keep learning. Again, don't be afraid to make mistakes; this is the best way to learn. Also, don't be afraid to ask the people you know if they need help. One of the best ways to master any skill is to help others, so you'd be surprised to find that you might have a friend or two who could benefit from your skills. Overall, Good luck and have fun.

About the Author

Roggie (Raj) Clark, is a 9 year SEO professional and owner of the SEO agency; *Bounce Rank.* Prior to joining the SEO industry, Raj was a web developer and school teacher. It was through creating his own websites, and wanting a career change from teaching, that Raj stumbled across the world of SEO.

Since joining the field nearly a decade ago, Raj has worked on a wide range of campaigns, from eCommerce, to B2B, to Healthcare, for enterprise companies and marketing agencies in the United States.

He is regarded as an expert, and guru by his colleagues, and the SEO industry. Raj currently lives in Maryland with his sister and niece.

www.ingramcontent.com/pod-product-compliance
Lightning Source LLC
LaVergne TN
LVHW082355200926
848481LV00012B/3576